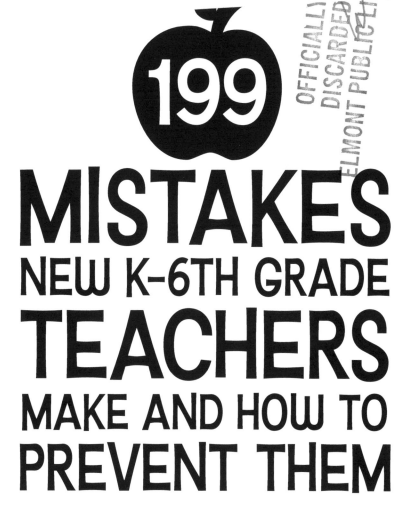

199 MISTAKES
NEW K-6TH GRADE
TEACHERS
MAKE AND HOW TO
PREVENT THEM

Insider Secrets to Avoid Classroom Blunders

KIMBERLY SARMIENTO

199 MISTAKES NEW K-6 GRADE TEACHERS MAKE AND HOW TO PREVENT THEM: INSIDE SECRETS TO AVOID CLASSROOM BLUNDERS

Copyright © 2017 by Atlantic Publishing Group, Inc.
1405 SW 6th Ave. • Ocala, Florida 34471 • 800-814-1132 • 352-622-1875 – Fax
Website: www.atlantic-pub.com • Email: sales@atlantic-pub.com
SAN Number: 268-1250

Library of Congress Cataloging-in-Publication Data

Sarmiento, Kimberly, 1975-
  199 mistakes new K-6th grade teachers make and how to prevent them : insider secrets to avoid classroom blunders / by Kimberly Sarmiento.
      pages cm
  Includes bibliographical references and index.
   ISBN 978-1-60138-621-2 (alk. paper) -- ISBN 1-60138-621-4 (alk. paper) 1. First year teachers--United States--Handbooks, manuals, etc. 2. Elementary school teaching--United States--Handbooks, manuals, etc. 3. Education, Elementary–Curricula–United States--Handbooks, manuals, etc. 4. Teacher effectiveness--United States--Handbooks, manuals, etc. 5. Classroom management--Handbooks, manuals, etc. 6. Lesson planning–United States–Handbooks, manuals, etc. I. Title. II. Title: One hundred and ninety-nine mistakes new K-6th grade teachers make and how to prevent them.
  LB2844.1.N4S27 2015
  372.11020973–dc23
                        2015002618

Printed in the United States
BOOK PRODUCTION DESIGN: T.L. Price • design@tlpricefreelance.com

Reduce. Reuse.
RECYCLE.

A decade ago, Atlantic Publishing signed the Green Press Initiative. These guidelines promote environmentally friendly practices, such as using recycled stock and vegetable-based inks, avoiding waste, choosing energy-efficient resources, and promoting a no-pulping policy. We now use 100-percent recycled stock on all our books. The results: in one year, switching to post-consumer recycled stock saved 24 mature trees, 5,000 gallons of water, the equivalent of the total energy used for one home in a year, and the equivalent of the greenhouse gases from one car driven for a year.

Over the years, we have adopted a number of dogs from rescues and shelters. First there was Bear and after he passed, Ginger and Scout. Now, we have Kira, another rescue. They have brought immense joy and love not just into our lives, but into the lives of all who met them.

We want you to know a portion of the profits of this book will be donated in Bear, Ginger and Scout's memory to local animal shelters, parks, conservation organizations, and other individuals and nonprofit organizations in need of assistance.

– Douglas & Sherri Brown,
President & Vice-President of Atlantic Publishing

TABLE OF CONTENTS

Chapter 3: Classroom Management 53

Keeping Control of Your Classroom...........................54

Avoiding Inconsistencies 66

INTRODUCTION

"The mediocre teacher tells, the good teacher explains, the superior teacher demonstrates, and the great teacher inspires," said William A. Ward, a poet, inspirational writer, and man of great faith, Ward points out what separated the teachers people remembered and loved from those who did not inspire their students in the classroom.

My friend recently posted a "throwback Thursday" picture of her and her father from our high school days. Since he has been deceased for a few years, she naturally received wonderful comments. While he was a great father to her – and to many of us, as well – he was also one of the greatest teachers I ever had.

Our families had been friends for several years, so I respected him in and out of the classroom. I believe he was a great teacher, but I might have been biased. It always warms my heart when I read posts about how he was such a great teacher and inspired his students to love math and science. Students did not just love him because he was a fun teacher—he taught them two of the most difficult subjects you could imagine in high school: physics and calculus. They loved him because he made learning fun and earned the respect of hundreds of students along the way.

Having a legacy such as his motivates many individuals to enter the field of teaching. From your first year to your retirement, where hundreds of students praise the impact you had on them, the journey is a long one. Furthermore, the classroom is a different world than even the one you learned in. Technology, standardized tests, parents, and even students are different. Some of the challenges you face will be different than your predecessors, yet some will be very much the same.

As a first-year teacher, whether or not you are able to inspire your students will likely be determined by a combination of your personality and passion, as well as a strategic effort to avoid common teaching mistakes. This book cannot help you bring things to your classroom that are not intrinsic in you, but it is dedicated to help you learn from dozens of seasoned teachers who once stood in your shoes.

The first thing you must understand about teaching is that it should be a calling, not just a profession. You have probably heard the saying "Love what you do and never work a day in your life." My advice, that teaching should be a calling not just a job, is not about any relatively false philosophy such as this. I love being a writer. My work spans several different genres, such as journalism, business, academic, technical and career development, and yet, I can assure you that there are days when my job is difficult.

Having first-hand teaching experience (on the collegiate level) and interviewing dozens of elementary school teachers, there will be days when it feels like the hardest and most unappreciated profession around, no matter how much you love teaching (nurses will, of course, vie for this title, but I believe it is a tight contest). "It is long hours and hard work, but it is all for the benefit of the students," says Sara Razaire of Volusia County Schools.

As a teacher, people will look at you as if your job is not *that* hard. You will hear comments about how you have more time off than other professions (an entire summer to kick back and relax!), and they will often assume your day ends when the school day ends.

Of course other teachers will express thoughts like this: "If you do not go home exhausted and spent, then you did not do your job," said Shay Matthews formerly of Tavares Christian School. But those not in the know may fail to take into consideration the amount of time you spend grading papers at home or preparing for future classroom assignments. Many people will also never realize that you will spend your personal dollars on school supplies. You might even notice numerous people making comments online about unreasonable demands by teachers for greater pay or benefits.

In addition to the general public, and perhaps even your friends failing to understand how hard your job is, how much time you spend at it, and how little money you really make at it (particularly early on), many parents will somehow forget just how difficult little Johnny or Sally is to manage at home. Despite the fact that parents will jokingly lament how their jobs grow exponentially harder with each additional child they have, even they can fail to understand how challenging it is to manage a classroom of 20+ students. You cannot necessarily expect buckets of sympathy from your students' parents; your job will be difficult, and it might even be thankless. Many people will not value or respect your work. You might even have to live with people questioning your intelligence, qualifications, and merit as a teacher. Have you heard the delightful saying "Those who can, do; those who cannot, teach"? You will have to live with all of this as well as excel in your classroom to succeed. This is not the recipe for a job someone gets because they cannot figure out what else to do. **This is the formula for a calling.**

If you are called, then this book is dedicated to making your initial foray into the profession of teaching as easy as possible. As the title denotes, this researched guide compiles 199 mistakes you should avoid as a new teacher for elementary-aged kids. Some of these mistakes might seem obvious, whereas others may be actions and attitudes you have not even considered. This book contains humorous anecdotes, stories from dozens of established teachers, and practical advice to help you succeed on the first day of school.

The book is broken down into three parts: **Classroom Mistakes to Avoid**, **Relationship Mistakes to Avoid**, and **Professional Mistakes to Avoid**.

The first section – Classroom Mistakes to Avoid – will deal with a wide range of classroom issues, such as curriculum development and managing distractions in your classroom. As a teacher, your classroom is the center of each student's educational development, so you need to know how to make it a happy place where you and your students can thrive. This section will help you plan what to do by detailing what *not* to do.

The second section – Relationship Mistakes to Avoid – is not about your dating or married life. As much as I argued that teaching must be a calling, I also want to emphasize how important relationships are in regards to your teaching experience. Your job will be much more than communicating information to eager sponges waiting to learn. The relationships you form with students, parents, and even colleagues will define your teaching career – for better or worse. Therefore, the second section will guide you in building good relationships and avoiding pitfalls that come from having "bad people skills." This section will also offer some solid guidance on how to deal with difficult people. No matter how great a teacher you are, not every student or parent is going to love you. Knowing how to deal – or at least how not to deal – with those who do not like you or who feel that you are not doing your job will help you succeed even in the hardest moments.

The last section – Professional Mistakes to Avoid – focuses on your professional development and how to avoid issues that will delay your career advancement. I would love to tell you that if you excel in teaching your students and managing your relationships well, then that will be enough to have a great career as a teacher. Just like professionals all around the country have to deal with politics, you will have to navigate through school politics. You will also have professional standards you need to meet, professional development you will need to complete, and career decisions to make along your 20- to 30-year career path. Since a great deal of my professional life is spent working with people who are seeking new employment and/or career advancement, this book includes important information to cover for new teachers. Therefore, the last portion of this book is dedicated to sharing stories from established teachers on how to gain tenure and stay employed in a world of budget cuts, restricted resources, and standards.

This book will help prepare you mentally for the issues you could face and develop strategies to overcome or at least bypass each of these 199 mistakes. If you must first learn in order to teach, I encourage you to learn from the mistakes of others shared in these pages, and enjoy your first days of teaching by avoiding these stumbling blocks to success.

PART ONE:

CLASSROOM MISTAKES TO AVOID

After completing your bachelor's degree, several teaching practicum programs, and required state certifications, you send your résumé to multiple schools with alacrity. After several interviews with multiple principals, you receive an offer to teach at a wonderful elementary school and prepare yourself for the beginning of your teaching journey.

As excited as you are to start your teaching career, you are likely full of questions and concerns, which led you to this book. The first section is dedicated to possible mistakes you could make in the classroom and how you can avoid them. Filled with content that ranges from classroom management, to curriculum development and delivery, to avoiding classroom distractions, the following chapters will focus on helping you in the classroom.

CHAPTER 1:
Before School Begins

Have you ever heard the saying, "an ounce of preparation is worth a pound of cure"? It is, of course, a common expression that promotes the merits of planning ahead; age-old expressions have so much basic truth to them. This one is credited to Benjamin Franklin and might be one of the most essential truths any teacher could follow.

As a new teacher, you will report to your "office" (i.e. classroom) well before the first day of school. You will have meetings, planning sessions, and even more meetings on top of that to learn about standard operating procedures, policy changes handed down by your school board, and general goals set by your school's administration. This process is important for you to familiarize yourself with your new school and get comfortable in your new role.

While you attend these meetings, getting to know your fellow faculty, and counting down the days until your students arrive, your classroom and curriculum planning needs to already have begun. No matter what grade you are teaching, you will likely have assigned curriculum and material you need to cover. It is your job to create and execute a lesson plan that allows you to go through that material in a timely manner and ensure all of your students have mastered it by the end of the year. While you will need to remain flexible, the process of lesson planning needs to begin weeks before the first day of school.

In addition to preparing class material, you will also need to spend some time working on the classroom itself, such as layout and general setup. Depending on the age of the students you are teaching, it might be applicable to decorate your room with bright colors and cheerful images that make the children feel welcome and excited about being in your classroom. You might also want to develop a seating plan and work on the room layout, so you are not making it up as you go on the first day of school.

While it is likely that your school will have a code of conduct, rules for your students to follow, and policies on discipline that you need to follow, you will have to decide what your personal rules for your classroom are going to be. It is advisable that you decide these rules, post them on your walls, and communicate them frequently to your students on a daily basis. This is an important area to focus your attention on before your students arrive, because you could be playing catch-up otherwise, and risk losing control of your classroom early on. For specific advice on preparation errors to avoid, read on:

MISTAKE 1:

Not defining the rules of your classroom before school begins...

If you are teaching kindergarten, you are probably aware of the fact that you will have to teach children the rules of school and your classroom. While many students attend preschool classes, there are some five-year-olds who are happily attending school for the very first time when kindergarten begins. Therefore, you understand you must guide these children not only in the material you need to cover, but also in what it fundamentally means to be a student.

Conversely, you should not think that if you happen to teach older children that they already know how to behave in school. Many – or maybe even most – probably know how to behave in the classroom (at least in general terms). However, some students will come from another school system, private school, or even home school. Additionally, not all teachers have the same rules or expectations for their classrooms. What you think is standard (for instance: not chewing gum in class), might have been permitted by other teachers.

In order to ensure students understand what you find permissible, make sure you define your rules for your classroom and communicate those to your students on the first day of school. *"Why would I need to do that?"* you might ask. *"The school handbook should cover all the rules, right?"* Simply put, the student handbook might not cover everything you need your students to understand for classroom conduct.

Some questions you need to ask yourself in regards to classroom conduct are:

- Are you going to be the kind of teacher who allows uninvited talking, or asks that a child raise his/her hand to speak?
- Are you going to allow the students to bring toys or other items from home, or prohibit such items in your classroom?
- What is your system for students to line up in order to go somewhere?
- Will you have assigned seats?
- Will you have classroom helpers assigned to certain tasks each day, or accept volunteers?

- How will students address a paper (with first name only, first and last name, name and date, etc.)?

- What do you want students to do when they complete an assignment or test?

It is important to answer these questions *before* the first day of school starts.

You also need to spend some time before school begins thinking about how an average day will go and how you want to structure your teaching experience. Try to imagine as many scenarios as you can – such as what a child should do when they need to go to the bathroom, or if they get cold or hot while you are teaching (can they stand up and put a jacket on or take one off) – and decide how you will handle these situations. Then prepare a way to communicate your policies to your students.

It will probably not take long for students to throw something at you that you did not anticipate or cover in your classroom policies. However, if you have done the prep work, these surprises will not overwhelm you, and your students will probably already have a good idea of what your reaction might be. Additionally, having established rules and policies will help you maintain order in your classroom, enrich the learning experience for students, and possibly prevent your nerves from getting frayed too easily.

MISTAKE 2:

Not defining what the structure of your day will be...

Some elements of your day will be decided for you: starting time, lunch time, when your class will go to specials, and when the day ends. However, you will be able to decide how other elements of your day go with your students. I am sure you will develop a plan as to when you will cover each subject you need to teach the children. Just remember as you map out your day to leave space for the little things like scheduled bathroom breaks or snack times.

If you have complete control over planning when you teach which subjects, try to create a schedule that will make your day the easiest while maximizing the benefit to your students. For example, it might not be best to schedule the hardest subject after lunch when you will need to recapture the focus of some children and ensure others are not getting sleepy after filling their tummies.

Also, as you work through the school year, if you find that something is not working, make changes. If these alterations benefit both you and your class, there is no reason to hesitate in making adjustments – just do not do so too often as it will confuse your students.

MISTAKE 3:

Not having a behavioral system setup and ready to use...

Within a couple of days before starting school, my children started coming home beaming and telling me they "had a gold-star day", which of course, translated to having great behavior in school that day. The color-coded star system is an excellent way for both children and parents to understand how well the child is doing in the behavioral parts of school. Reducing a child down a rank or color is also a good way for a teacher to communicate that the child needs to adjust their behavior in the future.

While these systems are a mainstay of kindergarten and other elementary school teachers everywhere, if you want a child to learn and respect it, you must communicate this on the first day of school and use it immediately. Children will learn quickly the downside of misbehavior and the benefits of gold stars.

Remember that communicating to parents what these colors represent is also vital to the success of the system. Sending paperwork home that you want a parent to look over and sign is an excellent way to make sure that parents understand the behavioral system you are using and what the results of bad behavior might be (i.e. getting sent to the principal's office, detention, loss of playtime). While not all parents are willing to read or sign paperwork, many will back up your good behavior system at home by rewarding gold stars for good behavior and penalizing poor performance days.

Of course, if you teach older students, the behavioral system needs to be adjusted, but the essence of structure needs to remain. A third, fourth, or fifth grade student still needs to immediately understand the consequences of talking out of turn, skipping ahead in line or teasing another student. Students need to be aware of the results of a first, second and third violation as well.

The first and second mistakes go hand-in-hand. No student should be permitted to claim ignorance as an excuse for poor behavior, or for not understanding what the consequence of his or her actions will be. Define your system and communicate it early on, so you will avoid being "tested" by students who cannot stop themselves from wanting to see what you are made of.

MISTAKE 4:

Not having a teaching plan for the first week of school...

You might believe that between communicating classroom rules and a behavioral system to your students that you will hardly have time to teach them anything the first week of school. Additionally, you still need to learn their names and instruct them about the ins and outs of daily school life (like when they go to P.E., eat lunch, and attend specials such as library, music, art, or computers). So how in the world will you have time to cover any school material?

You will need to make time to assess the children's academic progress and needs. This will be essential whether the children are beginning kindergarten or sixth grade. Understanding where your students fall in terms of reading, writing, and other academic abilities will help you adjust your earliest lesson plans, if need be. After all, there are few reasons why you should spend extensive time on material your students comprehend or skip over studies that students have not yet fully grasped.

If you start your academic lessons without these early evaluations and the children are missing skills you think they should have, then you will risk frustrating the parent and child as they struggle to catch up. But if you spend a week or two going over things your students already know, then you may bore them and make them disengage early. Furthermore, you might need that time later if the majority of your students need you to spend more time on a concept.

So, your first course of academic action should be to determine what your students already know. As you do that, you should also start to teach them some basic material. Even if you later decide to slow down or speed up the pace of lessons, getting students accustomed to school is as important as teaching them how to behave properly.

Therefore, the best advice for elementary-aged teachers is to have a plan that is highly flexible and adaptable for student performance as the year progresses.

MISTAKE 5:

Not spending some time setting up your classroom...

Teachers have some leeway in setting up their classrooms. Some classrooms have several themes that reflect the teacher's personality, as well as the students they teach. While this might be more inspiring for the younger grades, classroom décor can help create an environment that will make the students feel comfortable and engaged in learning right from the start.

For example, if you are teaching kindergarteners, it is important to make them feel like school is a welcoming place rather than a sterile, foreign environment that reminds them they are no longer at home. Older students might appreciate being engaged in school pride by having the room decorated in school colors or with a school mascot. This can help them appreciate the school as something that "belongs" to them and that they are a "part of" rather than it just being a place that they have to go.

Your classroom setup is more than just decorating your door or wall space; it is also about deciding the best seating arrangements, where students will store their supplies, have reading time, and more. When you look around your classroom, you will need to approach the planning like a foreman designing the optimal layout for a manufacturing operation. You should decide what space you want to allocate to which function and setup your classroom accordingly.

MISTAKE 6:

Not working a child's needs into your seating arrangements...

If you are going to assign seats, you need to decide how – alphabetical order, allow the children to select their seat and then remain in it – and then communicate this policy to the students. You will need to remain somewhat flexible due to changing student needs (like changes in eyesight or hearing) but knowing where you want your children to sit on the first day of class will help you bring order to your classroom right from the start. New students will appreciate the structure, and older students will respect that you have a system and appear to know what you are doing.

MISTAKE 7:

Not optimizing your floor plan...

Additionally, having a floor plan ready will allow you to answer questions from students and parents on the first day. When a parent walks their child to class to take the "first day of school" pictures, meet the teacher if he or she did not go to orientation, or drop off school supplies, they expect you to be organized and prepared to answer questions. Students will expect the same. Being "easy going" and "friendly" does not mean responding to questions about where to put a lunchbox with "oh, just over there, we will sort it out later." Parents will not be impressed and if a student has had a very organized teacher in the past, they might even question your capabilities. Some students might even see this as an early sign that they can put you to the test in other areas.

Having a specific plan for your classroom will give the appearance that you are in control on day one. It will allow you to confidently lead your students through the day and help them learn the routine you want them to adopt. Be flexible and capable of making adjustments if they are required, but make sure you at least look like you know what you are doing on the first day of school.

MISTAKE 8:

Not factoring safety issues into your classroom policies/rules...

I am sure many of your classroom rules will cover safety-related issues, such as when and how to use scissors, glue, and other school supplies. But it cannot be stated enough how important it is that you go over safety rules with your students. For the rules that are most important, you should have instructions on your wall regarding what to do and when to do it. Go over these rules on the first day of school and several times throughout the school year to prevent accidents or injury.

MISTAKE 9:

Not creating parent paperwork before school begins...

Parents of kindergarteners might be surprised by the vast amount of paperwork that comes home with their students in the early days of school, but the rest of the elementary school's parents are likely prepared to receive, read, and sign several pieces of paper for their child the first week of school.

Of course, the parents have already completed a handful of paperwork for the school, but it does not hurt to duplicate some of the questions in your own communications. Invite parents to tell you about food allergies, eyesight or hearing needs, and specific pick-up instructions if you like. Parents of children with allergies or special needs are far more likely to want to tell you that information than to be annoyed by having to repeat it.

You will also want to prepare documents that communicate your classroom rules to the parents and your behavioral system. If you want parents to support you at home, it is best if you explain your system to them early on – not when a student has to be reprimanded and cannot explain why to his or her parents. Other topics you might want to review with parents early on include:

- How you plan to communicate with the parents
- How parents can reach you and/or meet with you concerning their child
- Your grading policy
- An overview of the material you plan to cover on a quarterly, monthly, or even weekly basis
- A list of things a student is and is not allowed to bring from home
- If and when you plan to offer tutoring or help sessions

Of course, being able to communicate this information to your student's parents requires that you have thought it all out and made a plan before school begins. If you have done that, explaining it to parents early on will only be to your benefit. You should also invite questions from the parents and make sure you provide them a way to communicate with you – by email, at least.

One final note about early parent communication is to consider providing your students with a reward for having their parents sign portions of the papers you send home and return them to you. Create a tear-off portion of your classroom rules sheet, grading policy, and other paperwork. If the student brings it back to class signed by a parent, they receive a treat of some kind (i.e. candy, stickers, a trip to the treasure box, get out of homework pass).

The purpose of this reward is, of course, to motivate the students to share the paperwork with their parents and get it signed. If you fail to create a reward, too many students will throw the papers away without their parents seeing them or the parents will do the same. You want to provide an incentive for these documents to be read so your communication efforts can reap the maximum return for your efforts. You could put a negative consequence in place for the student not returning the signed paperwork, but that might lead to frustration if the student has a highly uninvolved parent. I would advise a reward over punishment so a student can only benefit from their parent's action, rather than be hurt by their inaction.

MISTAKE 10:

Not making the most of student orientation...

As part of your preparation for the start of school, you will be expected to participate in a student orientation several days before the first day of class. This will give you an opportunity to meet several students and their parents. Treat this meet-and-greet session as something more than just a chance to shake hands and connect names with faces.

First of all, this gives you an opportunity to hand the paperwork previously discussed directly to the parents. This may or may not increase the likelihood that it will be read and digested by the parents, but any chance you get to communicate with your student's parents is one you should take. Creating open dialogue early in the process should make things easier if you and the parents ever need to address a serious academic or behavioral issue.

The next thing you can do is to ask parents to fill out a little "tell me about your child" questionnaire. Some parents might not want to do this, but many parents would love to tell you about their little one and provide you with additional insight about their child prior to the start of the school year. Allowing them this opportunity will give you a chance to get to know more about your future students and perhaps even help you plan better for the first day of class.

If you have already decided your classroom layout – and perhaps even seating assignments – this will give you a chance to walk your future students around and acquaint them with your classroom setup. The more students who are familiar with and comfortable in your classroom on the first day of school, the easier it will be for you to bring the whole group up to speed.

Finally, this is an opportunity to connect with your parents and discuss things like school supplies and what the students need to bring from home on a daily basis. Even though they know that many teachers spend their own money on classroom supplies, parents can resent the amount of money they need to spend on school supplies at the start of each school year. Discussing what your students will need the most and what they will be using the supplies for can help bring the parents around. Just remember not to ask for anything truly extravagant if you can make do with something simpler. Parents probably would not like the idea of you spending your hard-earned money on crayons and paper, but they are equally unlikely to want to buy modeling clay when Play-Doh would suffice.

In conclusion, no matter what you elect to cover in your orientation session, remember to use it as a means to make your first day of school a better experience.

MISTAKE 11:

Not anticipating extra students in your class the first day of school...

Last-minute registrations are a given. For whatever reason, you will always have parents who register their children late or move into the area after the first day of school. Those students will need to be placed in a classroom.

Even the administration might not figure out whose classroom these children will be in until the first day of school. Therefore, you should be prepared to add one or two more students into the early roster you were given before the first day of school.

This means you should make a few extras of whatever handouts or work you are going to disperse. Be prepared to rearrange your seating setup if your added students need to sit toward the front of the class. Basically, be comfortable with the fact that your best laid plans might be at least partially swept aside for late additions to your student body.

If you have decorated your classroom with items that contain your students' names, quickly amend these things to include your last-minute additions so they feel at home and included in their new surroundings. This applies if you add a student on the first day of school or several days later. Remember that it can be difficult to attend a new school, so you should do what you can to make your new additions feel welcome – whether it is the first day, week, or mid-way through the school year.

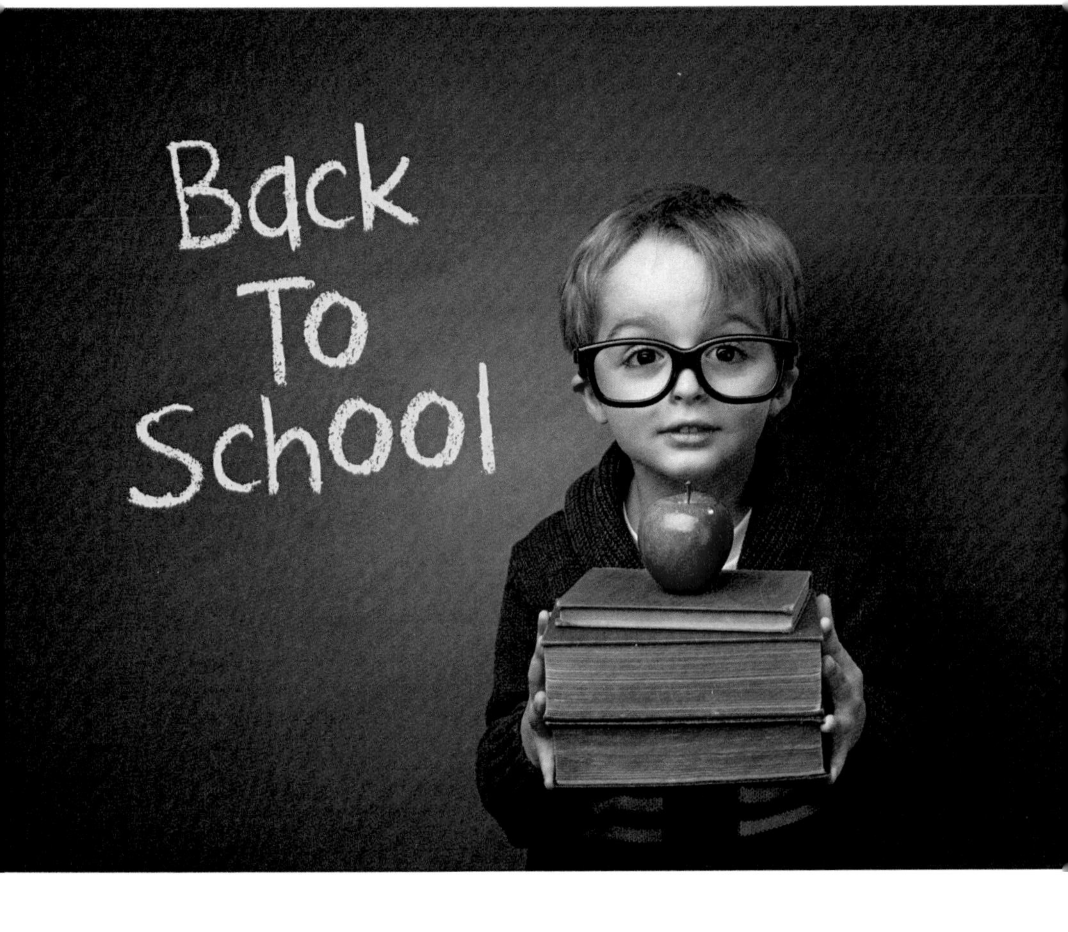
Back
To
School

CHAPTER 2:
The First Day of School

As a teaching assistant at the University of Florida, the best advice I was given was, "Be strict and firm in the beginning of the semester, and then lighten up later if you can." If I created a relaxed or even loose classroom environment early on, then I would have never been able to regain classroom control as the semester advanced. And in this case, I was teaching college-aged adults.

Most psychologists tell you that structure, rules, and routine are good for young children; so therefore, it makes sense for teachers of elementary-aged children to have strict rules for their classrooms and a clear system of enforcement. That is not to suggest that you can never have fun with the children you teach. But you should understand that if you prioritize "having fun" and "entertaining" the children, you will be in a situation rife with first-year teaching mistakes.

While you might not consider yourself a leader, you are, in fact, the leader of your classroom, and managing young children can be a task that is far more difficult and different than any other leadership position. Chapter 1 talked about preparation and how you can set yourself up for success before children storm your classroom and the chaos begins. Chapter 2 will focus on the first day (or first week) of school and how to launch the school year off on the right course by avoiding these common mistakes:

MISTAKE 12:

Making the first day all about "fun"...

I know I covered this in the first chapter in terms of preparation, but all the planning in the world will be no use if you do not implement it on the first day. While it is important to make your students feel welcome, you must immediately communicate the rules and expectations of your classroom and what the consequences will be if these rules are broken.

Since you have determined how you want your students to behave and how you want to structure their day, be sure to communicate these things to the children both verbally and by demonstration. If you make your first day all about "fun," you will miss an opportunity to cover rules and procedures that need to be reviewed, which will only delay how quickly you can get into teaching.

I know you want to make a good impression on the children and try to get them into the mindset that learning is fun. But whether they are excited or scared, your students are coming to school knowing they are supposed to be learning. Do your best to make them feel comfortable, but do not lull them into thinking the year is going to be easy. Make sure your students know that the school year is going to be challenging but exciting, and you will do all that you can to help them master the material as you learn about some really cool things.

MISTAKE 13:

Not keeping things simple...

Have you heard the acronym K.I.S.S.? It stands for keep it simple, stupid. The idea is that most systems work best if they are kept simple. This principle translates well for teaching children, particularly young children. Whether you are instructing your students on the first day of school or leading them through a series of tests, be sure to keep things simple and straightforward for them.

MISTAKE 14:

Not reviewing the student handbook with your students (at least the highlights)...

Do not leave it up to your students to fully understand a student handbook on their own. If you want to adhere strictly to the school's rules and policies, go over the student handbook with your students on the first day of school. Select parts of the student handbook you want your children to really understand and post them on your classroom walls. You can even give your students a little "quiz" on the student handbook to ensure they have read and understood the rules and policies.

MISTAKE 15:

Not instructing students on how to line up when leaving the classroom...

The school where my children began kindergarten had colored, painted lines on the sidewalks for the students to follow. The classroom had a line leader that was alternated daily, and the students walked along obediently where they needed to go even while teachers talked to each other or a visiting parent. The structure was setup and the children followed it without constant harassment by the teacher to maintain order.

If this seems like an easy task to you, then think back to the times when you have seen a frazzled mother of four walking through a grocery store trying to make sure her children stay with her instead of randomly tossing items into her grocery cart. Maintaining order among children is not as easy as you might think and travelling from point A to point B will be your first challenge in this regard. Keeping children orderly as they pass friends in the hall or notice any number of things that will capture their interest requires you to plan ahead a bit, be persistent in your correction, and communicate both rules and consequences for breaking those rules repeatedly. Achieve this early on, and your first year of teaching will be off to a great start.

MISTAKE 16:

Not telling students what you want them to do when they finish an assignment...

When a child is done with a worksheet, quiz, or test, do you want them to bring it to you and quietly sit in their seat until the class is done? Or do you want them to turn the paper over and wait until you collect the whole classes' tests? Whether you use one of these systems or something else, making sure your students know what to do is important, so there is no confusion as academic work kicks into full gear.

As I mentioned previously, it is important to assess your student's academic abilities and needs early on. Use these evaluations to instruct students on how you want them to address each paper (i.e. name, date), what you want them to do when they finish an assignment, whether or not they are allowed to talk while working, and any other rules you want to setup. This method will allow you to communicate these rules early on without having to impact a student's grade if they fail to comply. Once you believe the students understand your system, you can add in disciplining measures for not complying with the rules of your classroom.

MISTAKE 17:

Not telling students what you will do at the start and close of every day...

Each day of the first week of school, you need to make sure students understand what to do when they arrive and how to prepare for the end of the day. Both procedures are extremely important. You do not want to get calls from frustrated parents that their students left backpacks or clothing items at school during the first week. You also do not want to have a student attempt to ride the bus home when they are supposed to go to an after-school program. You can relax when all of your students are safely on their way home – until then, stay diligent and focus on helping your students figure out where they need to be and how they need to get there.

Of course, there are many other things you can cover with your students the first day/week of school; these topics were selected to get you thinking of how you can make the most of the first week. Parents and students often wonder why the school year begins in the middle of the week, and it is commonly accepted that they will not be doing much at school in those early days. But in reality, with or without homework and tests, you are still actually accomplishing a great deal – if you work at it. Making those early days too focused on "fun" and having the students "like" you can waste precious time and set the wrong tone for the year. Start strong and save the "fun" days for the end of the year when you and your students will need them the most.

MISTAKE 18:

Not knowing your students' schedules...

By the time students enter middle school and certainly high school, it will be their responsibility to know their class schedule and where they need to go throughout the day. When teaching young children, you will be expected to guide them through their day when they are not with you. You will need to know when your class goes to lunch and on what days they need to be in the library, gym, or music/art room. You will need to pay attention as these times change on early-release days.

Not knowing your students' schedule and being able to communicate it to both the students and their parents on the first day of school would be a highly unprofessional mistake. You should have it printed out for your reference and send it home for the parents to review. You particularly need to let parents know when children have lunch if your school encourages parents to visit their children at this time.

MISTAKE 19:

Not knowing if one of your students attends special classes/sessions...

In addition to knowing the schedule of your average students, you will also need to know if any of your students have special needs. Some programs require students to operate on a deviated schedule. These can range from gifted programs with accelerated reading or math specials to accommodating a student with physical needs or an I.E.P. plan.

Many of these special programs will not begin until the school year is underway a bit. Other students might need special accommodations right from the start. For example, if a student carries an otherwise normal schedule but does not participate in gym class, be sure you are aware of where the student needs to be during that time.

Sending your students to the wrong location at the wrong time will not create an air of professionalism for you with your colleagues, and the students might even notice your error. It is also probably a good idea to verify anything your students tell you about their schedules. While it is understandable that last-minute changes can occur and you might not have information that the student does about their special needs, you still do not want to create an atmosphere where you appear easily fooled. Be proactive in managing your students' schedules and you should be able to navigate the early days of the school year without any major errors.

MISTAKE 20:

Not knowing how your students will go home at the end of the day...

In addition to knowing where your students should be throughout the school day, it is also important that you know where they need to be as the school day comes to a close. In decent-sized public elementary schools, children might be picked up by parents in cars, use bicycles, walk home, ride buses, or go to after-school care programs. If a child takes the wrong transportation home, he/she can get lost, and the parent will panic.

If parents attend orientation, ask them to inform you then how their child leaves school each day. If not, ascertain that information from the parent as quickly as possible – you might even have to call them if the parent does not communicate with you early enough in the school year for your comfort. It is important to know where your students need to go and that they know where they need to go at the end of the school day.

Do not wait until the end of the school day to discover if your students know this information. As a first-year teacher, it is understandable that you are nervous and anxious on your first day of school. You might be so relieved to end the school day that you relax and let the students celebrate a little. While this might seem harmless, it could lead to carelessness when identifying how students will get home. No matter how tempting it might be to take a deep breath at the end of the day and exhale, wait until the children are on their way home to do this.

The last thing you want to happen is to allow a student to take the bus home when his or her parents mean to pick them up by car, or a student wanders off to an after-school program with a friend when he or she should take the bus home. Check with your students earlier in the day if they know how they are supposed to get home and verify that information with the school, if possible. If there is any confusion, use your lunch break to straighten it out. It is better to be overly cautious than have a student get lost.

MISTAKE 21:

Not evaluating your students' strengths and weaknesses...

As I previously mentioned, you will have students join your class at the last minute or even later. These students may have joined you from a different school system, a private school (or public school if you are a private school teacher), or a

home school environment. In fact, even the students you know you will have in your classroom on the first day of school might not have attended your school the prior school year.

Students from a wide-range of school setups might mean that your students had different learning experiences and will start the school year with different knowledge and skill sets. Outside of curriculum, there are other influences that could impact what your students know and what they need to learn, ranging from contributions by the parents to summer camp activities.

For these reasons, it is important for you to quickly assess and understand what skills, knowledge, and tools your students already possess and what they still need to master. The earlier you identify areas where your students might need extra help, the faster you can bring them up to speed and advance the whole class together.

Therefore, I recommend that you evaluate your students' abilities and knowledge the first week of school and adjust your curriculum however necessary to accommodate what you glean from these assessments. This should make your whole school year run more smoothly.

MISTAKE 22:

Not reviewing previous year's material...

Unless you have the privilege of teaching Kindergarten, your students are not new to the classroom or learning experience. They all come into your class with a perceived level of understanding they should have achieved the previous year. However, as all parents have experienced, the ability of a child to remember what we want them to forget and to forget what we want them to remember knows no bounds!

For this reason, either before or after you perform a skills assessment, you should plan several review sessions for your students. You can either conduct a review session first to wake their little minds up from the summer slump and then evaluate their skill sets when you think they are firing on more cylinders. Or conversely, you can assess what they retained and prepare your review sessions on what you learn. Either way, a review of basic math and language at the very least should prove valuable to advancing your student's mastery and performance in those areas.

CHAPTER 3:
Classroom Management

Whew! You made it through your first day of school – it should be all downhill from here. OK, not really. Putting student faces with the names on your roster was the easy part; now the work begins. The first thing you must realize is that whether you are teaching adorable little five-year-old kindergarteners or fifth and sixth graders on the cusp of their teen years, you will be dealing with personalities that are highly formed, but you can still strongly influence these children for years to come.

You must accept that they are largely who they are going to be without forgetting that you can still have a strong impact on their learning experience and desire to learn. Your best and worst moments may very well be remembered for decades to come, even when these children are grown and working in a wide-range of professional fields.

Understanding that you are important to these students without presuming that you can really alter their natural personalities is a vital step in ensuring your success as a teacher. At some point in time, you probably took a Myers-Briggs personality test and can tell if you are an ESTJ or an INFP or one of the other 14 personality types this test identifies.

However, you might be surprised to learn that there are dozens of personality tests that can be administered for children. From tests that will code a child as a lion, beaver, otter, or golden retriever, to those that will tell you if a child is choleric, sanguine, melancholy, or phlegmatic. I am not advocating one particular coding system over another or suggesting that you give your students personality tests. I am simply reminding you that much of a child's personality is determined from birth.

Therefore, the child in your classroom that is extremely talkative is probably not trying to drive you crazy, but is that way because that is how they process information. Another child who gets upset when stories do not have a happy ending or when you discuss tragedies such as the attacks on 9/11 might not be emotionally unstable, but just a highly sensitive child.

Throughout your teaching career, you will encounter personalities in children that gel well with your own and are easy for you to teach, and ones that grate on your nerves in a way you never would have thought possible. You must learn to manage and work with diverse personalities as a teacher because you will likely encounter them all. And through it all, you must remain the warden of your class and not let the "inmates run the asylum," so to speak. This chapter is dedicated to helping you manage your classroom no matter what.

Keeping Control of Your Classroom

In the second portion of this book, I will dedicate a considerable amount of space to the relationships you form with your students and if you want to be perceived as a hard/strict teacher or a pushover. However, I cannot in good faith discuss discipline in the classroom without going over some basic classroom management strategies for maintaining control over your classroom.

You probably already realize you will have problem students, which can range from a disrespectful child to the "class clown." Dealing with students who disrupt your lessons may be more difficult than teaching the material itself. You must manage outbursts with professionalism while taking steps to minimize how often these interruptions occur.

What you might not realize is that it is not just the "bad" students who can sidetrack your lesson; very good, curious students can do it as well. While I was too quiet and shy in elementary school to be this child, I am most certainly the mother of two such students. Either of my children could charm the heck out of a teacher while taking over their class – without really even meaning to.

When a child is naturally curious about a concept or lesson you are teaching, it is easy to get caught up in that teaching moment. After all, this is your dream! A child is engaged and really interested in what you are teaching them, they are asking challenging questions and seem genuinely interested in the answers. And frankly, you need to be able to leave your lesson plan behind for a moment or two when the class shows an interest in something and gives you an opportunity to go into greater depth.

However, as tempting as it would be to go off on a learning tangent every time the opportunity arises, you have to keep your lesson plans more or less on track. And if you deviate from those plans, it needs to be at your discretion when you feel it would benefit the majority of your students. The following are recommendations on how to keep control of your classroom when children become disruptive for any reason:

MISTAKE 23:

Letting "gifted" children direct the class...

Gifted or advanced students can run the gamut in their personalities; some will be shy and quiet while others will be very outgoing and talkative. Every now and then, you will run into one who is charming and curious and will be able to all too easily dictate how the class goes if you let them.

Assuming they are not rude little "know-it-alls" who think they know more than you do, you will probably enjoy these students in your classroom. You will enjoy the questions they ask and knowing that if you call on them, they will likely have the answer or at least something interesting to say. These students will likely make straight A's – or close to it – and will make you look good on tests and evaluations that could impact your job.

However, it is for the benefit of the entire class, that you not allow these students to become "teacher's pets." You do not want to appear to favor these students over others because that will hurt your ability to engage your entire class. Furthermore, while many advanced children find it easy to interact with adults, they still need to be able to function well among their peers. Being perceived as a "favorite" with the teacher may not benefit them with the other students.

On the other hand, you do not want to stifle these students or their desire to learn. Therefore, find ways to manage their participation in your classroom. Rather than ask if anyone knows the answer to a question, group the children together on "teams" and divide the students that are more likely to know the answers up so that each team will be able to take turns getting questions correct.

If you are lecturing or doing a presentation, tell the students to take notes and write questions on a note card or piece of paper. Then at the end of your presentation, collect the papers in a box and pull out five to discuss as a class. You can bypass any card or paper left blank and just address the questions you find. Once you complete this discussion period, tell the students they can ask you additional questions after school.

Employing these strategies allows you to control the pace and direction of your class while still engaging your more advanced students. Additionally, it protects them from gaining a "know-it-all" reputation among their peers that is not always desirable.

MISTAKE 24:

Letting "big" personalities overshadow you...

In the previous scenario, the "gifted" student might have a big personality, but they are not the only child who can overshadow you in the classroom. From the overly disruptive student to the "class clown" there are several "big" personalities that can seize control of your classroom if you let them. You need to identify early who these students are and make sure you have strategies in mind on how to manage these children so you do not find yourself trying to wrest control back from them later in the school year.

Children seek attention in many ways for a wide variety of reasons. All too often, adults overlook bad behavior believing that the children in question just need a little attention and everything will be fine. It would be nice to think that any child "acting up" in your classroom just needs a little positive attention and reinforcement, and if you give it to them, all will be well. However, that is not always the case.

It might not be your attention the child is seeking at all. It could be the attention of their parents, the focus of a girl or boy that they like, or just popularity among their peers. Some children might believe that if they can make the class laugh, everyone will like them. Or they could be using "clowning around" as a cover for hiding a learning deficiency, inability to read, or other things that make them feel inadequate.

You want to make sure that you both pay attention to the reasons why the individual child is behaving in the manner they are, and ensure that you use the proper discipline measures to not lose control of your classroom. A disruptive student might need to sit by him- or herself for awhile or be sent to the principal's office if they cannot be quiet. A student who is clowning around might need to be separated from his or her audience. If the class is not functioning well in the midst of one activity, you might need to change activities to calm your students down.

MISTAKE 25:

Making a child feel "small" in order to put them in their place...

Do not be tempted to try to "put a child in their place" with inappropriate comments or sarcasm. Even if the child is acting a little too grown up and doing their best to act like they are the one in charge, you settle them down without hurting their feelings or making them feel bad. In fact, perhaps the best way to demonstrate to all the students in your class that you are in control is to remain calm and professional while you work to restore order.

One thing to understand about personalities is that some people are predisposed to avoid conflict or be non-confrontational. If you know that you are one of these types of people, be prepared to be a little harder and firmer with your students than you would normally feel comfortable being.

Some kids will push limits and test boundaries just to see what happens. These children can be well managed if you establish rules, be firm in consequences, and be consistent with punishments. If you relent on a few occasions, these types of children might push back to see if you will give in again. Just make sure you always back up what you say – these children will notice when you fail to do so.

MISTAKE 26:

Being too hard on kids who talk too much...

While it is important to maintain control of your classroom, you should be careful about how you deal with children who are too talkative, particularly those who want to talk about academic subjects. If a child is whispering to a friend about their favorite toy or television show, that is the kind of talking you absolutely should silence.

However, if a child is talking about school subjects and asking questions, you need to carefully instruct them to be quiet and tell them you will go over some of their questions later. Many children are far too shy to answer a teacher's questions in class. Others are quick to raise their hands and always want to show how smart they are. You need to make sure you can engage the reluctant participants without stifling the natural participatory instincts of those who are willing to speak out.

Imagine that you have a naturally curious student who enjoys answering or asking questions and feels no awkwardness when it comes time for class discussion. However, this student is only eight years old and his personality is still being molded. Your harsh criticism of his tendency to raise his hand during class gradually creates a scenario where he does so less and less as the year goes on. By the end of the year, you notice he is not raising his hand anymore and has gone from being gregarious to quiet.

The lesson has stuck. The once vibrant, excited learner has become a student who is quiet and not likely to volunteer in class. He will meekly give answers when called upon in class by future teachers and he will continue to get good grades, but some of his enthusiasm for learning has been squelched. Would you want to be the teacher that made that impact?

Instead of forever being remembered as the teacher that made little Jimmy not want to raise his hand in class, you have the opportunity to teach the young man about situational timing – that there is a time and place for certain kinds of behavior and he needs to be patient and wait until the right moment to talk and ask questions.

If you have a student that is distracting you from progressing through a lesson by asking a lot of questions, try designating a question and answer or discussion period at the end of the lesson. Have your students write down their questions as they think of them and then they can ask any that you might not have covered once the lecture is finished. This will allow the "talkative" student a chance to ask their questions in an appropriate format while also learning about adhering to the structure of a classroom.

MISTAKE 27:

Mixing it up with the class clown...

If you are a bit of a jokester yourself, when a student starts cracking jokes or clowning around, you might be tempted to joke around with them. And it is certainly fine to tell some jokes and make your students laugh from time to time. However, you also need to maintain an aura of professionalism that lets the students know you are NOT "one of them."

I know as a teacher you want to be liked, and you might even be one of those adults that find "burping" and "farting" noises funny. On some occasions, your "clown" might even crack some very funny jokes. You may smile, but you should be cautious not to get caught up in the laughter of the classroom. It will be hard enough to regain control of a bunch of elementary aged children once the giggles take hold of them...it will not be easier if you are having a good belly laugh as well.

Also, if one of your students cracks a joke that might be considered "at your expense," you should be sure not to joke back using them as the "punch line." You should have thicker skin than your children can hope to muster. Do not take any of their jokes or comments personally and make sure you maintain the aura of a manager at all times.

Finally, be cautious of unintended connotations connected to some jokes. Ensure that any joke you do make does not have any negative gender, racial, or religious stereotypes included. Even when teaching children, it is best to err on the side of caution and not risk offending anyone. Remember, even if your students are not offended or miss the biased part of the joke, if they repeat it to their parents – and they will – their parents might get upset and contact your principal. It is just best to avoid this scenario all together.

MISTAKE 28:

Responding harshly to a disrespectful student...

Every generation has their "walked two miles to school, in the snow, uphill, both ways" stories. I believe another version of that is "if I said/did that, my parents would have…." Nevertheless, it is a common perception today that children are more disrespectful, they know swear words earlier than they once did, and they may be more likely to use them.

If that perception is correct, the probability that you might have a child or two talk back to you or perhaps even curse at you seems far higher than when you were a student. When a child speaks to you as if they were an adult, it might be very tempting to speak back to them as if they were as well. You should resist that urge.

When a child is disrespectful, you should remain calm, professional, and – above all else – in control. Whatever your policy is to deal with disruptive students, put those procedures into practice. Isolate the child quickly so his/her negative behavior does not spread to other students. And if you need to send a child to the principal's office, do so before the interruption gets out of hand.

Just be careful not to yell, curse, or insult the child in your efforts to establish yourself as the dominant personality in the room. You want to maintain control of the classroom and of your emotions. Doing so will ensure that the non-disruptive students respect you while showing the disrespectful student that he or she is not going to get under your skin or provoke you.

MISTAKE 29:

Overcompensating for your perceived shortcomings...

You have heard of the Napoleon complex, a type of psychological phenomenon that is said to exist in short people where they seek to overcompensate for insecurities caused by their short stature. I have heard of short female teachers who operated like little dictators because by middle school, their students already towered over them.

These teachers somehow developed terrifying reputations with their students. There were not liked or loved, but they were feared, which seems to have been the teachers' goal. At a glance, it appears these teachers are taking the philosophy of "speak softly but carry a big stick" a little too far.

If there is some area that you perceive as being a weak point for you, address it as best you can, but do not let it dominate your concerns. You should work to highlight your strengths rather than worrying about covering up your weaknesses. With a good amount of planning and preparation, you can shrink your weaknesses to a point where your students will not notice them.

Understand that your students walk into the classroom assuming you are in charge. While some of them might try to push the boundaries and see if you mean what you say, they still walk in expecting you to be the one they need to try to challenge – that automatically means they know your rolse is as the "boss" of the class. Your goal will be to maintain that image.

As a new teacher, you might be younger than many of the other teachers and parents you work with. Do not let that be something that makes you insecure. If you maintain your professionalism and do your job well, before long, no one will notice your age.

While your children will probably not be perceptive enough to realize if you are exercising a Napoleon complex or some version thereof, coworkers, supervisors and parents will notice. If you are too extreme, the very thing you think is keeping the respect of your students might cost you that of your parents and colleagues.

MISTAKE 30:

Letting bathroom breaks get out of hand...

Compared to the other subjects I covered in this chapter, managing bathroom breaks probably seems out of place. However, children love to push limits and if you are not careful, something as mundane as a bathroom break can completely derail your lesson plan for the day.

While you certainly do NOT want a child to have an accident in your classroom, a series of bathroom breaks should probably be viewed with a suspicious eye. You should try to make note of patterns that your students demonstrate. If a child always asks to go to the bathroom during the same subject matter – math for example – that might be a sign that the child's request is more related to the material and less related to their bladder needs.

On the other hand, a student might need to go several times in one day if they appear to have an upset stomach or other bowel issues. If a student who does not normally ask to go to the bathroom frequently starts making the request several times in one day, consider that they might not feel well and accommodate their needs.

Finally, pay attention to whether or not one or more students are asking to go to the bathroom at the same time on a repeated basis. Your students might be using this tactic as a way to catch a little "play" time when they should be focused on your class. Girls might be especially prone to this strategy. Try to make sure the same students aren't taking advantage of bathroom passes on a repeated basis.

In order to ensure that bathroom breaks do not interrupt your lesson too much, try to set specific times every day when you allow students to go. When children are older and changing classrooms, they can work their restroom visits in between classes. For now, you need to help schedule that time for them. For example, ask students if they need to use the restroom before you start a test or have a period of time when you allow the children to go to the bathroom after lunch. This will help minimize interruptions to your lectures and ensure your class runs more smoothly.

Avoiding Inconsistencies

One of the most common pieces of advice parenting magazines offer is that children need consistency. As clichéd as this guiding principal may seem, being consistent in your classroom will serve you well. While young children might not yet be racist or sexist, they are aware of their differences. To a child, having an odd color hair, wearing gasses, having braces or even being left-handed can make them feel like they stand out in a negative way.

If you allow yourself to be inconsistent in how you treat your students, you could alienate some of them without even realizing it. You know that not all children are created equal – some of them will be brighter than others, some of them will be more athletically gifted, others will be prettier, and some will just possess an air of likability. If you are being honest with yourself, you will like some of your students more than others. However, you can never ever show that you think of any student differently than another. You must make your students believe that you care about one thing – educating all of them to the best of your ability.

Along with avoiding inconsistencies in how you treat one student from another, you should avoid irregularity in how you manage your classroom. Certainly, there are many things in your personal life that can impact your work. It is acceptable to have some minor deviations in your day-to-day teaching efforts based on whether or not you are having a bad day or woke up feeling monumentally inspired with just the right idea on how to communicate a concept to your students. It is, however, a poor teacher who behaves erratically from week to week, enforcing rules one time while letting things slide another.

If you want your students to respect you, then follow your rules and demonstrate their best behavior; you need to condition them on what to expect. If you are unpredictable and they are left guessing as to what the consequence of an action will be, they might be unable to decide if the action is one they wish to take or bypass. Being consistent in how you handle the same situation with every student will help your students understand that you mean what you say and that you are to be respected. The following mistakes are ones you should avoid, even if you do not currently understand why. Consider the advice below:

MISTAKE 31:

Being relaxed one day and firm the next...

The way you manage your classroom during the year is the way your students will expect you to manage it all year long. If you begin in a relaxed manner, it will be difficult to become stricter later in the year if you do not have as much control over your classroom as you might like. If you joke and laugh with the students about poor behavior one day, the children in your class will expect you to always overlook such conduct. Letting small violations pass will only confuse students later if you try to enforce harder standards.

Furthermore, if you are strict for several days, lighten up, then become strict again, you will utterly confound the students in your classroom. You will leave them confused about how to behave and what to expect from you. While your change in teaching style and/or mood could be completely independent of the students and simply a product of your personal life, you will still leave the students wondering if they are somehow causing the changes you are demonstrating.

In the worst possible scenario, your shifting mood and teaching style could damage your ability to teach effectively. If you want to protect your ability to positively impact your students and communicate your lesson plan, you will want to minimize anything that could distract from the education process. Among many other things that could have a negative impact, your inconsistent behavior is at the top of the list. When students are left wondering how the teacher will act from one week to the next, they are not fully focused on learning. You will want to limit how often this occurs.

MISTAKE 32:

Showing favoritism...

As I have previously mentioned, you can go ahead and draw the conclusion that you will have favorite students. While a parent might be able to hold off from favoring one child over another if they have more than one, in a classroom with 25 students or more it is very likely you will have ones you like better than others. You might even have a child or two that you look at and think, "My job would be so much easier if they were all like him/her."

There is nothing wrong with feeling that way inside. The mistake you must avoid is showing your feelings of favoritism to the student and/or class. There are many reasons you should avoid favoritism, besides the clear lack of professionalism it denotes. You might want to consider that favor from you could turn into claims of racism or sexism if a parent decides to bring it to your principal's attention that you are not being fair in your teaching practice. So the first reason to avoid favoritism is that it could be used against you in a complaint.

The possibility that such a complaint could get out of hand – *Ms. Smith does not like black students; Mr. Jones does not treat the girls the same as the boys* – only worsens the professional hit you might take. Please remember that while most people realize that children and parents are capable of complaining for no reason—you are a new teacher. Your principal, administrators, and school board do not know you as well as a seasoned veteran. It is best to be cautious early in your career and avoid mistakes that could lead people to forming negative opinions of you.

Showing favoritism could also limit your teaching impact on your entire classroom. First, you could create over-confidence in the students whom you favor, enabling them to believe that they are "better than" or "more deserving" than their counterparts. Second, demonstrating favor to your students could lead some of them to conclude that you do not care if they master the material just as long as your "favorites" do. Always calling on one or two students because you know they know the answer could lead some students to stop trying to answer questions or feeling too embarrassed to volunteer. You must strike a balance between rewarding those students who perform well and propping up the children in your classroom that need extra assistance.

MISTAKE 33:

Showing dislike for a student...

On the flip side of the same coin of favoritism is showing disdain for any one student or group of students. The first thing you should probably ask yourself is if you do have any preconceived ideas about people based on race, gender,  and religion. You should ask yourself if you are prepared to teach children of all races, religions, and even sexual orientations.

Depending on the size of the town or the area of the country you live in, the diversity issues you will encounter in your classroom could vary significantly. But the chance that you will teach minorities of any and all kinds certainly exists. You will encounter students with diverse belief systems, cultural norms, and gender identities, and you will need to maintain a level of professionalism in your classroom (protecting these students from bullying and harassment), while not communicating any negative, private thoughts you might have about the individual students.

The above scenarios might be at the edge of extreme, but they are certainly worth considering. A likely possibility is that you will simply have children in your classroom that you dislike. Perhaps little Johnny is rude or little Suzy is bossy and all of your attempts to curb this negative behavior have failed. You could have the misfortune of having a bully in your classroom and while you are able to control his or her behavior, you are unable to get them to interact with the other children in a positive manner. You could have a child who never turns in homework, does poorly on tests, and just does not seem to care about anything you are trying to teach.

Regardless of how much you dislike a student, do not show it – not to the student or class. The first thing you should keep in mind is that even if you do not reach that student in the first month or several months of school, you could still make an impact by the end of the year. Do not rob yourself of the victory of teaching a child that others would give up on. But you must also hold up the most difficult, problematic child in your classroom as an example to all the others. If you care about that child, then you care about them all. This is a message that your students will pick up on and internalize whether you realize it or not.

Of course, my warning not to show dislike to a student does not suggest that you should not discipline a problem student. However, this is about avoiding inconsistencies. When a problem student breaks the rule, handle him or her in the same way you would if any other student did so. Do not be harder on some students and easier on others. If you operate your classroom in a consistent manner, students will be less likely to pick up on who is your favorite student and worst nightmare. Approach the parents in much the same way, and you will build yourself a reputation for being fair and just, as well as a good teacher.

MISTAKE 34:

Using sarcasm...

Alright, if sarcasm is a second language for you, you are not going to like this section much. Heck, it is not my favorite talking point either. In fact, when I first read Katie Hurley's "Want to Stop Mean Girls? Raise Nice Girls, Instead" article and I got to that particular piece of advice, I rolled my eyes.

Then I thought more about what she was saying and I read the article again. Hurley is a Child and Adolescent Psychotherapist and wrote this article about her efforts to start a "friendship club" among fourth grade girls at the school where she was working. This was a response to teachers asking her for help with female students whose relationship troubles with each other were interrupting the classroom.

The program was successful and one key element she cites is eliminating "cutting comments" between the girls. If this is effective between elementary-aged children, it will be effective in your effort to relate to your students.

First off, students will not always understand your sarcastic comments or that you were attempting to be comedic instead of insulting. This misunderstanding will undoubtedly lead to difficulties as you work to impart your lessons to the class. Whether the student is just hurt and does not listen to the rest of your lesson or the student thinks you meant something else entirely, you will have failed in your communications with one or more of the children in your care.

Instead, say what you mean in a clear and concise way. Be patient with a student who is sarcastic or "smart" with you, and do not respond in kind.

CHAPTER 4:
Discipline Matters

Let us assume that you have already decided what the rules of your classroom are going to be and have defined a behavioral system to explain to your students the first day of school. Now you must address the ever-difficult task of deciding how to discipline your students when the situation warrants.

In all likelihood, your school has some discipline standards established, such as detention for skipping class or sending students home for wearing inappropriate clothing. More serious offenses like fighting or bullying might earn suspensions. Those disciplinary steps will be easy for you to follow.

However, there are smaller offenses that you have to decide how to handle. When a student talks out of turn or causes a disruption in your classroom by clowning around, you must decide if such behavior will earn the student a trip to the principal's office or after-school detention. You must decide if you will have a warning system and what it will be. As you figure these things out, do not hesitate to consult your fellow teachers to see what they do in their classrooms. If you watch enough examples and receive good advice, then you will be able to sort out what works best for you.

In the meantime, as you seek to develop your discipline policy, there are some things you should remember NOT to do; these errors range from disciplinary action you should never use to things that will just give you a headache if you do not avoid them. This chapter is dedicated to covering how to maintain control of your classroom while avoiding a wide-range of disciplinary mistakes.

Ways Not To Discipline – Ever

There are many mistakes you can make your first year of teaching (and even beyond) that may affect you professionally. However, there are a few that will likely get you fired or at least reprimanded by your superiors. It should be your highest priority to avoid committing these mistakes. Read below for the mistakes that are related to discipline:

MISTAKE 35:

Using ridicule to get a child in line...

If you have a sarcastic personality or caustic sense of humor, it would be easy to make snide comments when one of your students gets out of line or responds poorly to a question asked in class. As natural as that is to you, I highly recommend that you avoid engaging students in this manner.

There are several reasons why you should avoid ridiculing a child in class. The first is that it is more likely to cause you to lose control of your classroom than to keep it. Students will laugh at almost any joke you crack – at least all of the ones they understand. When laughter breaks out in your classroom, calming the students down will take some effort. If the students are laughing at another child, what little control you have left will evaporate if the student you made the snide comment to reacts in anger or tears – both of which are possible. Whatever you hoped to achieve with your comment – if you thought about it at all – will probably not be accomplished, and there will be negative results.

The second thing that will happen after a snide comment is that you will seriously damage your professional image with the students and parents who hear about the incident. The last thing you need to do is allow one small comment to injure your reputation as a professional. If you were working at an office among other adults, you might be able to make a snide comment without consequence if you do not let it happen very often, but students will not understand and neither will their parents. Once you have lowered their opinion and respect for you, it will be difficult to regain confidence and control of your classroom. Teaching and relationship building will become more challenging and some parents will be looking for other signs that you are not doing your job well. Basically, you will stack the deck against yourself and make your job harder than it needs to be.

If you are tempted to ridicule a child to stop them from making fun of or teasing another child in your classroom, you should think twice about adopting such tactics. While this might seem like a good way to defend the child who is being teased and could serve to make the "bully" understand what it is like to be laughed at, it is far more likely that you will only create an atmosphere where you drag yourself down to the level of the children you teach. The older your students are, the more damaging this could be to your ability to lead your classroom effectively. Once your students start to think of you as being "one of them" or "on their level," you have basically lost your ability to be their leader. In instances such as this, it is far more important for you to set an example of how to handle a "bully" with self-control than try to put the child in his or her place using ridicule.

In addition to the damage you can do to your relationship with your students on the whole, you will permanently fail the student you ridiculed. Whatever reason you have for wanting to bring the child back in line with a snide comment, you must not overlook the fact that it is your responsibility to teach all of the students in your classroom. Disciplining a student who disrupts your teaching allows you to send a message that your instruction is important, and you are not to be interrupted. Ridiculing a child sends another message altogether: it conveys the idea that the lesson is not important, and you are willing to abandon your teaching to speak condescendingly to one of your students. While that student might not act out again, he or she will not likely seek your help if he or she needs it for fear of more ridicule. Furthermore, other students might be equally unlikely to ask for help because they do not want you to make fun of them. This means you have not just damaged your ability to control your classroom; you have damaged your ability to effectively do your job.

Finally, it is not wise to use ridicule or snide comments to try to get a student to perform better academically. If a student answers your question with a smart remark or even an incredibly stupid comment that shows they were not paying attention to what you were saying, your job is to keep your composure and not make the child feel dumb. As in the above scenario, making a child feel stupid will not just decrease the likelihood that one student will feel comfortable participating in class – it will lower the chances that any of your students will want to respond to your questions.

Furthermore, you must not respond to a question from a student in a snide or negative manner. You may think that the saying "there are no stupid questions" is completely false. There are, in fact, many stupid questions, and you will probably hear dozens of them throughout your first year of teaching. No matter how much a student's questions make you wonder if he or she is even listening to you talk, you cannot answer them in a sarcastic or mean way. You have to remain professional and address their questions completely, no matter how tedious this task can be. If you do not adopt this philosophy, your students might stop asking questions – even when they do not understand the material. If they stop asking questions, you might find yourself wondering why they are performing badly on homework and tests. Maintaining an environment that encourages questions and learning will be the key to your success. Do not sabotage yourself with a sarcastic or snide comment – no matter how funny it sounds in your head.

MISTAKE 36:

Cursing...

Almost every parent understands how easy it is to lose your temper with his or her children, especially when it comes to yelling or cursing at them. Of course, just about every parent who has done this realizes that losing composure with a child does not gain you respect or make the child more likely to obey you. Simply put, while yelling and/or cursing might seem like a good way to let off steam and let your students know you "mean business", this will demonstrate poor professionalism.

Whether cursing is acceptable in an office setting varies on the office, the company, the manager, and the words that are used. A four-letter word at one company might not get you in trouble, but could land you in sensitivity training at another corporation. Cursing at work could negatively impact the impression you make on your boss or potential clients. When I advise clients in career management, I tell them to completely avoid it in an interview and limit it as much as possible in a new position.

In a school environment, you need to completely remove curse words from your vocabulary – particularly when working with young students.

I admit that it is unlikely that a child has never heard curse words before, and some of your students might be more likely to use curse words than you. However, it is still the essence of a professional teacher to avoid the use of vulgar language at school.

If a parent hears you curse or brings it to your principal's attention that you are cursing and yelling at your students, you will almost certainly earn yourself an official reprimand. If you say a curse word that could have sexual or sexist implications, you might receive a significantly more serious punishment. As long as you are the new kid on the block, avoid using language that will make your principal wonder if he or she made the right choice in hiring you.

MISTAKE 37:

Yelling...

You might be thinking, "Ok, I can raise my voice without cursing. Then the students will know I mean business without me getting myself in trouble."

You could use this approach, but I think you will find children do not respond well when adults lose their composure. Young children want to know the adult in charge of them is in control of the situation; screaming and yelling does not convey control of your classroom. Older children will lose respect for you once they learn they can get you riled up and off track from teaching. Some of them might even try to make you upset on purpose just because they know it is possible.

Keeping your composure in the classroom is about more than just maintaining professionalism or not giving parents a reason to question your qualifications to do your job. Remaining calm and restoring order in your classroom, even when things start to get out of hand, is about making sure the students know you are always in the lead. When you calmly handle a mounting situation without letting it rile you, students can see that you are in control of the classroom, and they will respond accordingly.

One of the most important ways you can keep control of your classroom, without getting to the point of losing your cool and yelling at your students, is to not let little things mount up. When you ignore small issues of misbehavior or let little things slide, some students will continue to test you to see how far they can push before you respond. If you address misdeeds early on with increasing forms of discipline as the offense increases, you can let your students know you mean business without reaching a level of frustration that will lead to yelling and screaming. So be sure to address issues early and not let them build up. This should help you remain calm and professional even as students test the limits of your patience.

MISTAKE 38:

Getting physical...

School spankings are more or less a thing of the past. Even in Catholic schools, you no longer hear about nuns hitting children with rulers or any other form of physical punishment. If you are of the "spare the rod, spoil the child" thinking, understand that there are many, many reasons that schools have backed off corporal punishment and it is best for your career that you follow suit.

First, for students old enough to have been subject to physical punishment in school, it often ranks among their worst experiences with teachers. Stephen Klubock, a Career Coach and Account Manager (who happens to also be a military veteran), described his two worst teachers as his third grade teacher who would hit her ruler across their knuckles and his second grade teach who would shake them in the supply closet to get them in line.

Decades later, he remembers those teachers not for what they instructed, but for how they behaved. The obvious lesson to be imparted here is that you do not want the only reason some child remembers you is because you back-handed them for ill behavior.

But the argument against getting physical with a student is stronger than not wanting to make a lasting bad impression. There is also the fact that what parents consider acceptable in terms of physical punishment varies widely, and you do not want to do something to a child that a parent might consider abusive. You can rest assured that 99 percent of time, it is best to keep your hands off the child when it comes to discipline.

On the very rare occasion where you might be called on to restrain one student from hurting another, you should still avoid physically striking a student. Not only could this behavior hurt you professionally, but in the litigious society you operate in, this form of discipline could get you sued. Slapping, pushing, or hitting a student is just not worth it, no matter how bad you might think they deserve it. If it comes to this, remove the child from your classroom immediately and give yourself and the rest of your students a chance to calm down.

Small-Time Discipline Measures

You understand the importance of maintaining control of your classroom and you are well aware of the fact that you will encounter behavior for which your students need to be punished. The previous section details some big

mistakes you should not make. And of course, you can rest assured that you can send children to the principal's office for major offenses such as fighting, bullying, and suspicion of substance abuse. However, you still might be confused, unsure, or even worried about how to handle minor disciplinary issues.

You have several options available to you on the disciplinary front when it comes to minor disruptions and student mistakes. There are times when a stern look, a firmer tone of voice (commonly referred to as your "teacher's voice"), or any number of other symbolic gestures that you have trained your students to recognize, can serve as a signal to be quiet.

In the moments when your students are more wound up, (such as days when they know there is going to be a class party or almost any day during the month of December) you might have to alter your lesson plan and engage your students in an activity that will capture their attention and tie into the subject you are trying to impart.

When you must use disciplinary tactics for one or two students, do so in a way that disrupts your class as little as possible and be sure to focus your correction on the child's behavior not them. I say this to help you build a positive relationship with that child overall, but also to ensure you will be able to work with the child's parents if the need arises. Read on to familiarize yourself with some mistakes to avoid when disciplining students for minor classroom offenses.

MISTAKE 39:

Sending students to the office
over small matters...

As a new teacher, you might be unsure about when to send children to the principal's office and you might even be tempted to use the experience to get problem students to straighten up. You also might think that if you have gone through your color-coded behavioral system, sending a child to the principal's office is the appropriate next step, regardless of the seriousness of the offense.

You should keep in mind that a referral to the office should be a serious disciplinary step and you will bolster your creditability as a classroom manager if you do not use it over small offences. Consider putting the following student errors on a "do not send" list for your students:

- Not doing homework
- Marking on desks
- Making rude comments or talking excessively
- Being occasionally tardy
- Not doing class work or failing to pay attention
- Chewing gum or eating in class
- Sleeping in class

For many of these issues, you can handle them in-class or after school. You can quietly wake a child up or ask them to throw their gum away. You can address a student being tardy with the child and then the parents if you are concerned their tardiness will have a negative impact on their studies.

A stern look, being separated from other students, and/or detention might be enough to get disruptive or talkative children to behave. In regards to those not doing their homework or class work, you can dock their grades accordingly. If you are concerned about them failing, contact their parents and schedule a meeting. As long as the student is not disrupting the class, the lack of effort might not be something you can change, but it does not necessarily mean a trip to see the principal either.

MISTAKE 40:

Not knowing your school's unexcused tardy/absence policy...

I may have just cautioned you not to send students to see the administrator for being occasionally tardy, but I also have to remind you that most likely – your school has a policy on how many unexcused tardy and absent days they will tolerate before there are negative consequences.

In some areas, if a student misses too many school days, they cannot advance to the next grade level regardless of the quality of their work. There are schools where too many tardy markings will count as an unexcused absence. You should monitor these markings and let the students and their parents know if they are in any danger of the attendance – or lack thereof – causing them to fail a grade.

You should also know when your school will expect you to refer a student to the principal for habitual tardiness. Just be sure to follow your school's policy so that if something comes up later, you cannot be considered culpable in the student's ignorance in the matter.

MISTAKE 41:

Using classroom control measures that could cause more disruption...

At any given moment, young children can burst into uncontrollable fits of laughter and silliness and it seems these fits are more contagious than the common cold. When you want to use a single method to get your children to be silent and settle down, be sure not to use one that could cause the children to become more rowdy.

One example might be if you are teaching in an enclosed classroom without windows, you should probably not use the "blink the lights" strategy to get your children's attention. This tactic works in a classroom with a lot of windows because you can still see your students. However, once the entire classroom goes completely dark – even for a second – any amount of silliness (or bullying) can ensue.

Do not put yourself in a situation where you could lose further control of your classroom. Examine your classroom and try to put yourself in the mind of a child. If there is the potential that your "control" method could make things worse – or if it does once you employ it – try something else.

Punishment that Might Create Resentment

While I have and will continue to emphasize that trying to be your students' best friend will not help you maintain control of your classroom, there are some disciplinary measures that will create unnecessary resentment. The "mistakes" I detail in this section may – at times – seem like a good idea. Just make note of the possible downsides and if you decide to employ these strategies, be aware of the potential results.

MISTAKE 42:

Using group punishment...

If you are teaching young children and the class starts to get rowdy or loud, it is certainly effective to use a "time out" measure that will settle the class down. These tactics could include blinking the lights in your room, telling all of your students to put their heads down for a minute, or having everyone hold up one hand while putting a finger to their lips in a "be quiet" motion.

However, beyond these "settle the class down" situations, punishing the class as a whole for the bad behavior of a couple of students will win you no respect. First, students cannot be expected to police one another and young children can hardly leverage positive peer pressure to keep the class in line for you. In fact, if a student does speak up to try to get the class to behave, they could be labeled a "teacher's pet" or "brown-noser."

Besides the fact that group punishment places the burden of creating good behavior on the students, it also creates a "you" against "them" dynamic in the classroom. While you do not necessarily need every student to love you, it should not be your goal to be seen as the children's adversary either. When you create this dichotomy in your classroom, it will make it more difficult for you to reach out to students who need help and to reward students for their achievements.

Finally, in the group punishment scenario, students will recognize that you are unable to get the few students under control who are causing the disruption. This will consciously or unconsciously lead to the students losing respect for you. Furthermore, if the students believe they will be punished anyway, rather than continuing to behave well, they might decide to join in the bad behavior of the initiators.

MISTAKE 43:

Assigning extra work as punishment...

While there might be a time and place to use this strategy, generally speaking, I believe that giving extra work to the class as punishment for the negative behavior of a few – or even several students – is a mistake. First, both class work and homework should be thought of as a tool for learning. Teaching your students that their work has another purpose – a negative one at that – could undermine what you should be trying to accomplish, which is teaching them that learning is fun.

Additionally, your students likely have a fair amount of work to get through without extra work. Assigning this type of punishment could adversely impact a student's ability to complete their assignments and get good grades. The last thing you want to do is make it harder for your students to excel in your classroom. Doing so will lead many of your students to stop caring and stop putting in their full effort.

Finally, the extra work punishment – particularly when assigned to the entire class – has all of the downsides of the group punishment mistake. You will do more to earn your students' respect if you show them you can deal with disruptive students and minor interruptions without punishing the innocent in the process.

The one exception to this policy is not really when you need to assign "extra" work, but if the class has been derailed enough – the class work might need to become homework. Your students are less likely to see this as a punishment and more as a result of the classroom disruptions. While they might believe you should get the rowdy students in line so they do not have to do their work at home, they will understand that they are not being asked to do anything above and beyond what you already had planned for them.

MISTAKE 44:

Forgetting to reward good behavior...

While you need to have a discipline plan in place and be prepared to use it to maintain control of your classroom, do not forget that one of the best ways to encourage good behavior is to recognize it, point it out to the class, and reward it.

You need to take care not to call any one student out too much in order to avoid the appearance of favoritism, but all of your students will exhibit good behavior at one time or another. Even your most disruptive child will do something you can praise if you look for it. Take those moments to reward the child for their good behavior and reinforce the idea that they can receive attention for being good – not just being a clown.

Try to remember that children are disruptive for a whole host of reasons. You do not necessarily need to identify the motivating factor behind a child's misbehavior, but do remember to use the "carrot" along with the "stick." When you praise a child who normally only gets noticed for acting out, you might see them try to earn your attention for positive action instead of negative action. If successful, this tactic could go far towards turning around their school performance and your classroom management.

CHAPTER 5:
Teaching Facts, Skills, & Concepts

When teaching elementary-aged children, you are not just instructing them on historical data and mathematical facts to memorize. You will be teaching them concepts and valuable skill sets as well – hopefully ones that they will carry with them during their entire academic career. Concepts can be complicated while skill sets will vary from the basic 123s and ABCs of Kindergarten, to study and testing habits as they age and work becomes more challenging.

Teachers communicate many facts to their students, from rules of grammar to the year Christopher Columbus sailed to the Americas. They help children memorize definitions, names, dates, formulas, the names of state capitals and more. These facts do not require critical thinking or analysis. Children do not need to deduct anything to regurgitate these facts on tests.

I do not mean to belittle the teaching of facts. In the time I spent teaching American Federal Government, I did quite a lot of communication of facts to the adult students in my classroom. Furthermore, my tests did require my students be able to answer questions based solely on the facts and figures they memorized over the course of the class.

However, much of teaching is not just communication of facts. It is instructing students in a diverse set of skills, including critical thinking. Facts can be memorized, but skills must be learned and then put into practice. You cannot just memorize how to read, you must practice reading to become truly proficient. Furthermore, you must be able to analyze what you have read to learn the skill of implicit reading comprehension. Helping your students learn this skill requires more than just practice, it involves discussion and debate and engagement.

When you instruct students on concepts, you will be helping them not only answer the "what" question of learning, but you will be tackling the ever elusive "why" question. I confess to being the anomaly in parenting, because I would humor the "why" question until we got to a point where I thought the explanation was beyond my child's understanding. This could be a matter of tackling a scientific concept that I was just unable to explain at the time, or it could mean that we had reached a point in our conversation where I thought visual aids would be needed to go any further. I do not know yet if my indulgence of the "why" game was beneficial to my children, but I believe as a teacher, you will be expected to follow in my footsteps and help students finally get their "why" answers.

Concepts teach children how things relate to one another or how processes work. Instructing students on photosynthesis is about more than teaching pure scientific facts – it involves showing students how nature ties together. When you instruct students on the parts of the flower and explain to them how pollinators move the process of pollination and help flowers reproduce, you are not teaching just facts to memorize. Students need to see how these concepts tie together in order to truly understand the subject matter.

This chapter is dedicated to mistakes that can be made when teaching facts, skills, and concepts to students, and how to make sure your students are getting the most of each category of learning.

MISTAKE 45:

Being opposed to re-teaching facts or concepts you feel students should already know...

Students learn certain skills each year of elementary school and they must be proficient in certain abilities to advance to their next grade. If your school expects students to master their times tables and long division by the end of fourth grade and you teach fifth graders, do not be surprised if you have to review the concepts after the long summer break.

When speaking with your students at the start of the year, and you are met with nothing but blank faces when you start using words like "prime numbers" and "consonants," you might be tempted to throw your hands up in the air and wonder if these kids know anything at all.

But after spending some time in the trenches of tutoring, I can attest that speaking to children about math facts and rules of grammar is a little like speaking to a person learning a foreign language. After taking French for two years in high school, I decided to advance my skills in college and take a couple of semesters there as well. I can still remember my Parisian French professor looking at me after a few class sessions and saying "Où habitez-vous?"

Required to speak only in French and not having any idea what she was saying, my only available response was "Je ne sais pas." This is of course my favorite French phrase, and if you cannot guess what it means, it translates to "I do not know."

Now going back to the original question the professor was asking me, it translates to "Where do you live?" Did I know where I lived? Of course I did. But despite the fact that she said the phrase several times, I could not understand what she was asking. Interestingly, when she became a little frustrated and wrote the phrase, I was able to understand it and excitedly replied "J'habite un Etats-unis!" Not a perfect turn of phrase, but it was fairly close to "I live in the United States."

My French skills have not advanced much beyond this level and I was always able to read and write French better than I could hold a conversation. But the point of the story is that until I could see the phrase written, I was hopelessly clueless. Your students might know what you are talking about if you jog their memories a little first.

Basically, after a summer of video games, swimming pools, and super hero movies, you have to get your students once again speaking the same language you are using. So, before you make a note to speak to teachers from the grade below you, try some board exercises or visual aids. The results might be somewhat reassuring.

However, even once you get your students on the same page as you, some of them still might not remember the skills they learned the year before. If they forget, it is your job to bring their skills back up to par so you can progress them toward more advanced skill sets. Therefore, any time you tackle a new subject, be prepared to review the basics before you get into the meaty part of the lesson. If you find some students in need of extensive remediation teachings, consider offering them after-school assistance.

MISTAKE 46:

Not reviewing after shorter school breaks...

You may understand the importance of review material after a long summer break, but do not overlook the need to review a little after holiday breaks such as Thanksgiving, Christmas, and Spring Break. Anytime a child closes their books for a week or more, there is at least some possibility they will forget the material you covered before break.

In fact, you can almost consider it a given that your students will not remember anything you covered prior to that break well enough to test on it. Do your best to schedule section tests prior to long student breaks. If you need to administer a test after a break, spend some time reviewing the material with the children and make sure they are capable of doing well. Save the joy of getting slammed with an exam after a week or two off for their high school experience.

MISTAKE 47:

Expecting transfer students to be on the same page as your regular students...

This book is being written amidst the turmoil surrounding "Common Core" curriculum and the corresponding effort to develop a standardized teaching practice across the US. Concurrently, there is a counter argument that children learn at different speeds, and trying to fit them all into one mold is quite damaging to their development.

Of course, one of the reasons the proponents for a standardized teaching curriculum arose to begin with is that from state to state and even school to school, what a student learns can vary greatly. This creates an environment where if a student transfers into a school they could be lagging behind or advanced beyond their peers just because their old school moved at a different pace than their new one.

Whether or not we ever achieve a common thread in our education system between the states, teachers must simply accept that a transfer student might be at a different point than the children entering their classroom having attended the school the year before. As a result, you need to be prepared to meet those children's needs and adjust your plan a little to either catch them up to your class or keep them engaged while you cover material they already know.

MISTAKE 48:

Thinking a student is slow because they
are lacking a certain skill set...

Whether or not a student came from another school or just did not master a skill set they should have before coming into your classroom, you should recognize that an inability in one area does not equal a lack of ability across the board.

While most people recognize that adults are good at some things and not others, we do not necessarily recognize this fact in children. Even when students reach the high school level, an honors or gifted student will be encouraged to take advanced courses in every subject. The simple fact is that a student might be well qualified to take advanced science, but should only be in an average-level English class.

Since this book is targeting teachers who instruct elementary-aged children, my advice is to not conclude that a student will be good in everything just because they are good in some things. Nor conversely should you believe that a student is slow if they are struggling in one subject area. Try to recognize your students' strengths and weaknesses and help them where they need it while challenging them where appropriate.

MISTAKE 49:

Grouping students according to ability...

On the surface, separating groups according to their demonstrated skill level might seem like a good idea. In this manner, if a student excels in reading but is lacking in math skills, they will be with advance students for reading and the slower students for math – allowing a child to be challenged according to their current capabilities.

The problem is that some research indicates this type of segregation in the classroom only benefits the stronger students without creating the "extra support" the slower students need. It is reported that teachers often have lower expectations, demands, and tolerance for the slowest groups of students and the quality of instruction for these students decreases.

Some researchers suggest that because students possess academic strengths and weaknesses, grouping children in slow or advanced groups can lower their self-esteem unnecessarily. Instead, supplementing a child's lagging area with peer-tutoring or after-school help can allow the student to catch up in their weak skill area without the perception of being labeled "slow" or "stupid" (Mason & Good 1993).

CHAPTER 6:
Curriculum Strategies

I wish I could tell you that if you can manage your classroom well then teaching will be easy as pie. I also wish I could tell you that the coursework you covered while completing your degree prepared you for every situation. The truth is that there are several challenges you will face during developing and communicating course material to your students; you might be aware of some challenges, and others could come as a surprise.

These challenges include trying to achieve the balance between creative/blended learning methodologies and preparing students for standardized tests. You could face difficulty in finding ways to engage bored students, challenge advanced students, or get frustrated when students fail to grasp the material you are trying to teach quickly enough.

Developing curriculum that will teach your students all the lessons they need to fulfill academic standards for their grade level might seem fairly straightforward at a first glance. However, using visual, audible, and hands-on learning techniques, while keeping yourself flexible so that you can speed up or slow down as needed, might not be very easy to do your first year of teaching.

Even though you are the teacher and prepared yourself for years to teach, you still have much to learn – and you will learn new things each year as each new group of students comes in. You have to learn about your students, what they know, what they need help in, their strengths and weaknesses, what engages and makes them love learning, and even more. In order to make the most of the school year, you must learn these things about your students early while remaining flexible as new discoveries are made throughout the year. Please review the following mistakes and see what lessons you can learn from them.

MISTAKE 50:

Teaching as if only standardized tests matter...

In states such as Florida, the idea of "teaching for tests" has become the bane of teachers everywhere. The instinct of legislatures wanting to measure the success of teachers or schools makes some sense, but the execution of tying school funding to test results has created an atmosphere where students feel tremendous pressure to do well on tests, and teachers feel like they must prepare children to achieve results that will get them ranked as an 'A' school.

While legislative policies cannot be changed easily, this book addresses why falling into the trap of "teaching for tests" will do you little good during your first year of teaching or ever. If you fall into the category of teaching a year that is measured by state tests, you might feel a great deal of pressure to make sure your students can do well on these exams—but ignore it.

This might sound extreme to suggest that you should ignore this impulse because, of course, these test results are important, but I can assure you that teaching strictly for these tests will not make your students more prepared than if you just cover material in a natural manner that works for your classroom.

Throughout the year, you will have to introduce your students to the process of standardized testing – such as not talking while taking tests and filling in answer forms properly – but you can work that into a normal testing scheme. You can even make learning to fill in answer forms a classroom or homework activity where the purpose is to color in the bubbles fully and neatly – not answer hard questions.

Approach standardized testing with the mindset that it should just be an evaluation of your teaching, not the point of your teaching. You can instruct your students about all the materials they need to learn without boring them or making them feel more pressure than what is necessary for the testing process. Furthermore, you will feel better about going to work each day, which can only enhance the learning experience for your students.

MISTAKE 51:

Teaching as if tests do not matter...

As much as I just said that you should not teach for tests, you cannot ignore the fact that these tests have real-world implications. While you should not adjust your entire curriculum to center itself on these tests, you need to keep in mind the elements of such tests that will be different for the children in your class.

For example, there is a good chance that your students have never used a Scranton answer sheet prior to this academic year. In order to ensure your students' tests are graded accurately, you will need to teach them how to fill in the answer sheet neatly and completely. As I have pointed out earlier, you can likely make this a fun classroom exercise rather than make it a mundane activity before every test your students complete throughout the year.

Other ways you can prepare students for standardized testing is to implement rules early on that they will need to follow during the test. You might need to warn them that they cannot talk during tests for any reason or instruct them to sit down with a couple of sharpened No. 2 pencils so they do not have to get up during the test.

I recommend starting out lightly at the beginning of the semester to introduce these concepts – i.e. give five extra points on a test if the student is sitting at their desk with sharpened pencils ready to begin at the start of class or deduct points if a student is caught talking or asks to go to the bathroom in the middle of a test. Then you can strengthen the consequences of not following these rules as the semester advances.

MISTAKE 52:

Being too hard on children who do not test well...

When it comes to preparing children to take standardized tests, I caution against a "zero-tolerance" policy early on because many students might not be used to the rules that apply to this form of testing and should be given

some time to get accustomed to following them.

When my daughter was in third grade, she faced a zero-tolerance policy like this at one point. I had studied her spelling list with her and I knew she was prepared for her test. So naturally when she came home with a zero because of "cheating", I was very concerned.

I spoke with the teacher via email and she explained that this had happened because my daughter had been caught talking. According to my daughter, another child had asked her a question and she answered. Since I was completely confident my daughter was not asking for or giving help, I asked the teacher if there was anything we could do. My daughter was allowed to take a harder version of the test and have it count for her grade – and she passed without issue like I knew she would. She was just unfamiliar with the classroom rules and needed an adjustment period. While nothing like this happened again, I still remember thinking it was harsh for the start of the school year.

Again, I believe you should place a focus on preparing students for these tests, but do so slowly and without placing more stress on the students than needed.

MISTAKE 53:

Getting frustrated with students who are not grasping the material and aren't ready to move on...

Many teachers think that once a lesson is taught, it is time to move on to the next area of study. If a student or several students are lagging behind or not grasping the material, you might feel frustrated and tempted to move on and just let that material slide. While I understand that you have much ground to cover in a school year and are concerned about how the students will measure up if you lag too long in one area, it is best to be flexible with your curriculum.

If you are only losing ground with one or two students, then you can offer special tutoring to help those students catch up. But if students do not understand the lesson, then you need to take some extra time to communicate the lesson effectively. Perhaps you need to try to convey it in a new way or just spend more time working with each student one-on-one until most of your students catch on. Just remember, there might be times when your students move through material faster than you thought and things will balance out.

MISTAKE 54:

Ignoring bad or bored students...

As a new teacher, if you have a student who is performing badly, you might be motivated to provide them extra help and work with them to raise their grades. That is an excellent instinct, and many sections of this book will address how to do that and also mistakes to avoid so you do not get overwhelmed.

However, on the opposite end of the spectrum, if you have a student who has a bad reputation or is acting disinterested in your instruction, you might be inclined after awhile to leave them alone. I want to caution you against giving up on such students; even a little effort can go a long way to get a child to pay attention in class.

Christian Langley, a current stay-at-home dad, taught high school history for several years and recently told me about an experience he had with one particular student who was performing poorly. Chris said he was sitting in a parent-teacher conference listening to the other teachers and when it was his turn to talk, he had to say that his experience with the student was not the same. He said the student was not an A student, but he performed well enough to earn a solid C in his class.

Chris told me that one of the biggest differences he noted between himself and some of the other teachers was that he would get up and walk around the room when the students were working silently at their desks or taking tests or even during his lectures. He said that it is surprising how well a student will wake themselves up and focus when you stand beside their desk for a few minutes.

I believe the lesson behind this is that you can engage your less-inclined students as well as your best performing ones. It is okay to call upon a student who you suspect is too scared to participate in class or create activities that all students can contribute to. Get up, walk around your room, and ask the students if they have any questions individually. These small steps can encourage participation and develop a relationship needed to help a bad student turn things around.

MISTAKE 55:

Not engaging students who are more advanced...

On the opposite end of the spectrum are advanced children who might not need your help at all. You will likely have some little star in your classroom – hopefully several – who eagerly soaks up all of the knowledge you have to impart to him or her. Little Suzy or Jimmy will get almost everything right, raise their hand to answer questions, finish their work without your help, and just be really easy for you to handle.

You will likely consider such students heaven-sent during the hardest lessons you have to teach, but do not make the mistake of ignoring these students and not challenging them. As the mother of a daughter who can be restless in the classroom and a son who is overly talkative, I know how important it is for teachers to keep good students occupied even while they seek to work with slower ones.

If your school has a gifted or advanced program of some kind – i.e. Math Super Stars, Advanced Reading Programs – see if you can qualify these students for the extra workload. That will go a long way to keeping their minds active as you spend time with your students who are struggling to master the material. In lieu of such programs, you can assign them additional reading time or have them help you with classroom tasks such as sorting crayons or passing out papers.

You need to avoid the appearance of favoritism because singling out students in the wrong way can pose problems on this front. However, you can balance efforts to keep advanced students busy and engaged without having a "teacher's pet".

MISTAKE 56:
Using words or language your students do not understand...

As a parent, I never engaged in the practice of "baby talk" or talked "down" to my children. However, I did encourage them to ask questions if I used words they did not understand and was ready to use a synonym to explain a word if my vocabulary exceeded their understanding.

While you want to expand your students' vocabulary – and will undoubtedly do so over the course of the school year – you probably do not have time to stop your lesson every time one of 20 plus children misses your meaning. As a result, you should try to use words your students will grasp easily while making sure you repeatedly use the vocabulary and spelling words your class is studying each week.

CHAPTER 7:
Tests & Homework

Homework and tests are an important part of your curriculum as well as quizzes, classroom participation, presentations, book reports, and various other methods you can use to evaluate if your students have mastered the material. It is important that the means you use to assess your children's understanding of the subjects you teach is properly designed for their skill level while employing several different methodologies.

Not every student will test well. Some will do better on certain types of questions (multiple choice) than others (essay). Be sure that when you design tests and homework assignments, you make sure you are not using just one method of evaluation. Also, ensure that your methods are appropriate for the age you are teaching.

The most important thing to remember is that you can change your methods as the year progresses. If you try something and it does not seem to work for any of the children in your classroom, be open to altering your lesson plan accordingly. Read on for more specific discussion on both homework and testing mistakes to avoid.

The Great Homework Debate

From the time I was a child until today, there has been an interesting change in how parents schedule their child's time and how parents feel about homework. I do not know if I have been blessed with incredibly adept children or teachers who do not assign a plethora of busy work or both, but I have rarely had to share the sentiment I see and hear about the horrors of homework.

Furthermore, while I believe there is merit to organized sports, social events, and even extracurricular activities such as music lessons or martial arts, I do not believe that children need to be overscheduled every night of the week. I am a parent who believes that school comes first and other activities should be peppered into a child's life as academics permit. After all, school itself still offers numerous ways for children to be enriched – i.e. art, music, languages, and more – within a structured day. The options only expand as children age, too.

So I commiserate with any teachers who believe that parents are over-scheduling their children and transforming extracurricular activities into academic distractions. Still, there is research that supports the idea that homework volume has increased over time. A University of Michigan research study of thousands of school aged-children ranging from 6 to 17 reports that time spent on homework increased from 2 hours and 38 minutes to nearly 4 hours since 1981 (Hancock 2011).

A couple of hours of homework each night is probably fine for a high school student, but it will be too much for most elementary-aged children, especially younger ones. Furthermore, other research studies suggest that the correlation between homework and academic achievement is nominal during elementary school.

The sentiment against homework and criticism of testing measures – from teaching to pass standardized tests to tests that are ill-designed for the way some students learn – is only exacerbated when a parent looks at the homework or test and finds it to be ill-conceived (like many opponents of the common core profess) or when parents help a child do hours of homework that's not graded for content but merely recorded having been done.

There are few things that are more frustrating than to do something that feels like it has no point. As the coach of any team will tell you, practice is vital to prepare yourself to face and overcome a challenge. Homework – or practice testing – has a place in academics, and testing is important to measure students' progress and success. However, there are mistakes you can make in creating and assigning these, and those mistakes could lead you into conflict with parents.

MISTAKE 57:

Giving "busy work"...

If you do not want parents cursing your name, then do not assign homework that is just "busy" work. I understand that you believe practice work is good for students, and you probably record a homework grade if the students do their work and turn it in, but if you are too busy to correct the work – do not assign it. It is just that simple. If you find yourself just checking off work without reviewing it in class with the students, you are likely assigning work that does not need to be done and infuriating the parents of your student in the process.

I still remember sitting down with my fiancé's oldest son and trying to figure out why he was struggling with math. I was very surprised to see that he was doing his math homework wrong and hear that his teacher never pointed that out. His teacher was giving him a homework grade for doing the work, but not reviewing it in class or checking to see if it was done correctly. And let's face it: practicing something the wrong way is a quick path to failure.

If you practice playing football without learning the rules of the game and it comes time to play, you could find yourself unable to advance down the field due to penalties. To achieve success, you must practice following the rules as much as completing a pass or a run.

When it comes to homework, it is not enough that students do the work you give them just for a homework grade. If that homework is going to benefit the student, then it must be reviewed so the student can learn what they did wrong and how to fix it. I believe too much homework for elementary-aged students falls into this "busy work" category, which is why students are not learning anything from the process.

My advice is to give homework that will be followed-up the next day in class and assign homework that the student was unable to complete that day. If you are teaching reading, have students read at home and discuss the passage in class. If you are teaching math, convey the lesson, do some practice problems together, let the students do the work at home, and then review it together the next day. If you have students write sentences at home for spelling or vocabulary words, assign your students to read and share them in class to vote on which ones were used the best.

Remember that as important as your time is, you do not want to overwhelm yourself with grading; students and parents need to feel like their time is not being wasted either. So all homework assignments should have meaning and value. If it is nothing more than a check mark, you and the students can probably do without it.

MISTAKE 58:

Giving too much homework...

Once students enter middle school/high school and have different teachers for their core subjects, the simple truth is that you are going to end up with an overload of homework one night or another, or all your tests scheduled  on the same day. A middle school and high school student has to plan ahead, work hard, study, and learn valuable organizational and time-management skills along the way.

But elementary-aged students are not, at this point, fully aware of the learning process yet. Therefore, you have it in your power to not overwhelm them. You can break up tests and stretch them out over several days. You can free your students up from homework the night before a big test. You can create your schedule in such a way that makes things easier on your students. This will go a long way to prevent parents and students from feeling as if you are giving too much homework or just abusing your students with busy work.

MISTAKE 59:

Not allowing more than one day to complete homework...

When it comes to helping students not get overwhelmed with homework, another bit of advice I can offer you is to give students a few days to complete all assigned homework. One of the greatest things my son and daughter's kindergarten teacher did was give them homework packets to work on each week that matched  what they were doing in class. These packets would come home on Monday and need to be returned the following week. They included several practice pages on letters, math, reading, and writing; in total, it was quite a bit of work. However, they could do them in any order; we could do three pages one night and skip a night if we got busy and make it up later. The format provided flexibility and allowed me to plans things out and I never felt resentment for the work we did together.

MISTAKE 60:

Assigning homework that is too hard for the students to do alone...

I strongly believe that homework – for the most part – should be something that a student can complete alone. While it is very important that parents be there to answer their child's questions and assist them with concepts and lessons they cannot understand, homework should not make the parent feel like they themselves are in school again.

When children are learning to read is an obvious exception to this policy as the children need to be able to read the words and make the sounds of the letters for someone to know they are doing their practice work correctly. Even still, that homework is not so hard the child cannot do it alone – it just requires a bit of supervision.

For every complaint I read from a parent about their child having too much homework, there is a correlating complaint that **they** are spending hours of the night doing homework with their children. For some families, it seems that homework time has replaced family time! That should not be the case and I cannot see how this helps children learn.

The homework you assign should not cover material you have not reviewed yourself in class. Homework should be a review of the lesson you covered, not a preview of lessons to come. If students feel like they know – or are at least familiar with – the material they are covering in their homework, they can both complete it faster and not feel frustrated while working on it.

I recommend that you remain flexible in your homework assignments. If you do not fully cover a lesson in class, tell the students they will have an extra day to complete their homework. Additionally, if the students do not seem to be grasping the lesson in class, cancel or extend the homework assignment until you have a chance to review it with them again. Remember, practicing something the wrong way serves no purpose.

Homework should be practice and reinforcement of something a student has learned – not a way to rope the parents into teaching something you have not completely covered in class. Remember that homework is for the student – not the parent. Assigning a student homework that they cannot complete on their own will only frustrate them, turn them off the subject, and annoy the parent that they need to explain something to their child that you did not.

QUICK REVIEW: When it comes to homework for elementary-aged students, which of the following is TRUE:

A. You do NOT have to assign homework every night of the week.

B. You CAN give students more than one day to complete a homework assignment.

C. It is ok to cancel a homework assignment if you think your students are not ready for it.

D. All of the above

MISTAKE 61:

Assigning tests or homework without paying attention to the school schedule...

By the time students reach high school – perhaps even as early as middle school – many are completely convinced that teachers actually pile on assignments and tests deliberately. Whether or not this is true, as the primary teacher in your classroom, you have the opportunity to manage your students' homework and tests schedules so they do not get overwhelmed.

First, if it can be avoided do not assign homework or tests in all subject areas on a single day. You can space out your assignments so students have adequate study and preparation time in all areas. It can also be helpful if you schedule certain tests or quizzes on certain days of the week. For example, a spelling test every Friday and a math test or quiz each Wednesday. That level of predictability will help students learn to plan ahead.

Next, you should pay attention to holidays and school events when assigning work. For example, you might not want to schedule a test the day after the night of the school Christmas event. Finally, if you scheduled homework and/or tests on a day that turns out to be bad for the students, be willing to adjust your schedule. While you cannot be completely accommodating to everything that comes up throughout the school year, you should try to give your students their best chance for success.

Fair Testing

You will always have students who believe your tests are too hard or unfair. You cannot throw out test scores or accommodate every complaint. However, you can take steps to ensure you are conducting your testing in the fairest manner possible. Make sure your tests incorporate different ways of asking questions and be willing to throw out a question if most of your students get the answer wrong. Consider the following mistakes you can avoid so that no one can falsely accuse you of being unfair in your testing.

MISTAKE 62:

Giving tests that only leverage one way of learning...

As an extension of the concept that "teaching for tests" is a bad idea, giving tests that only use multiple choice or true/false types of questions that fit well with standardized tests might fail to completely measure what your students have learned.

When I was creating tests for my classes, I tried to blend as many different types of questions into the tests as I could. Some students actually do better at short-answer questions or essays than true/false, where others do better with multiple-choice answers than fill in the blank. In order to provide all of your students with a chance to excel, it makes sense to leverage multiple styles of testing/question construction.

Furthermore, some students might not do well on tests at all but are good at making oral presentations or preparing poster boards on a special subject. You need to incorporate these types of opportunities when teaching, particularly older elementary-aged children. However, even kindergarteners can draw you a picture illustrating something they have learned.

Allowing a young child to draw and color pictures to illustrate a math concept might seem unusual, but it could give you a means of understanding what the child knows and does not know, and which you may not see on traditional tests.

Just remember that being creative and flexible in how you test, question, and grade a student will allow the majority of your class to express what they have learned and give you a better understanding of what material your students have mastered.

MISTAKE 63:

Not using a "curve"...

I am a big believer in giving the grade that the student earns. In other words, I do not advocate passing a student who has not reached decent subject mastery just so they do not have to deal with the shame of being held back. However, when I make a test, it is not a fool-proof process. When no student achieves an "A" on a test or very few students achieve a passing grade – there was clearly a failure in the preparation given the students or the test itself.

No teacher should feel reluctant to provide some kind of "curve" on his or her tests. My fiancé's daughter had a teacher who graded the tests and then returned them to the students, allowing them to open their books, correct the answers they got wrong, and receive partial credit back for their corrected work. I think this is an effective way to assess what the students know and allow them to learn from their mistakes.

Conversely, you can spend some time evaluating the test a bit and identify if there were questions that all (or most) of the students missed. In that case, you can review the question and see if you think it was badly worded, or something you did not cover sufficiently in class. If you identify any, throw those questions out and re-grade the tests accordingly. Finally, you can just use a simple curve where the highest grade becomes an A or a 100 and adjust all grades from that point.

The important thing is that you realize that students talk to each other (and so do parents), and giving them tests where no one succeeds does not make you a "hard" teacher who demands a lot from their students – it makes you look like a bad teacher who is not doing their job. You do not need to "go easy" on your students so you are well liked, but you do not want them to feel like an A is out of their reach or that success is unachievable either.

I think this is an important matter for new teachers to understand because, most likely, you have just come from a collegiate environment. Since the time I completed my master's in political science at the University of Florida, I have maintained a large network of college professors. We all know that teaching methods for college professors range from "relaxed and easy" to "sadistic." If you have had one – or more – of those professors that starts their class year off stating proudly that they have only given three A's in 20 years, your idea of grading and "curves" might have been skewed in the process.

Try to remember that these are children, not adults, and success needs to be within their grasp. Do not be afraid to adjust your grading scale, use a curve, or provide extra credit to empower their success.

MISTAKE 64:

Creating overly complex tests...

It is highly unlikely that young students will ever be able to understand the nuances of test questions that are looking for the "most correct" answer. Frankly, elementary-aged children might not be able to correctly answer any question that has more than one correct answer. Therefore, "all of the above" and "none of the above" answers might confuse them.

When writing true/false questions, consider the age of your children as you decide how complex they will be. While the standard rule for true/false questions is that "if any part of the statement in false, then the entire statement is false," that is a concept that is more easily understood by older students.

For questions with an answer bank, make sure your students know if an answer can be used more than once or if they can expect all of the terms from the answer bank to be used. Providing pointers like that to your students should help them complete the test with greater success.

MISTAKE 65:

Not allowing enough time for students to complete a test...

Of course you cannot allow your students to spend hours on any one test, but do make sure you are not following some "minute per question" ratio your children are not up to meeting. Be sure to spend ample time explaining the instructions for a test and let the children  know how long they will have to complete it. If it seems like very few students have turned the test in when it comes time to collect the tests, you might want to give your class a little more time.

When you look over the test results, if it seems like the majority of your class was unable to finish or struggled with the end of the tests (in other words, they guessed), reevaluate how long you make your tests. While you cannot adjust your plans to suit every child in your classroom, you can make note of how most students are doing. If most students are doing poorly, you probably need to make things easier in some way.

Identifying & Dealing with Cheating

Cheating is probably not something you look forward to dealing with in your classroom, but you should definitely have a plan in mind for how to address the issue if/when it arises. If you think drawing a hardline on cheating will discourage the behavior in your classroom, you are probably correct. However, be sure that you correctly identify the student who is guilty of cheating and hand out a punishment that is appropriate for the offense.

MISTAKE 66:

Punishing the wrong child for cheating...

When my daughter was in third grade, she came home one day and told me she had her spelling test taken away from her because she might have been cheating. I received no note from the teacher and I knew my daughter would have aced the test if she had been allowed to complete it because I had reviewed the words with her all week.

I contacted the teacher and asked what happened. The teacher explained that my daughter and one of the other students were talking during the test and she had to take the tests away from students who talked on the assumption of cheating. Thinking back, I cannot remember if this was the teacher's policy or the school's because as she explained to me, this was being done in preparation of a state-wide standardized test that was being administered at that grade level.

The students had to practice their testing as if they were taking the big standardized test later that year, which would be strictly administered to prevent cheating. Since the results of these tests can impact the funding that school's receive and even a teacher's job security, I certainly understand why teachers and schools must prepare students on how to take such tests.

However, negatively impacting a good student's grades because someone speaks to them and they reply is not good policy. Fortunately, the teacher had enough flexibility to offer my daughter (and the other student) a make-up, harder version of the test. She easily made an A and learned a lesson about talking during tests.

My caution for new teachers would be to follow this example in one sense and learn from it in another. The only thing I think this teacher did wrong was not either explaining to her students that she would permit the make-up test automatically or sending home a note explaining to the parents what had happened and that there was a make-up option.

Otherwise, if you need to have a highly strict policy about talking during a test, permit a make-up option for students who are not cheating. Even if it is a harder version of the test, allowing students who engaged in a conversation that might have had nothing to do with the test itself to receive some grade is better than penalizing them with a zero. Furthermore, when one student talks, it could be to tell another child to keep their eyes on their own paper or to "shhh" someone who talked to them.

Assigning blame for cheating during a test or quiz is likely not a cut and dry issue and an innocent student can easily get caught up in your discipline measures if you are not cautious. Be sure to listen to the students and communicate with the parents. Permitting a "make-up" option for a first offense should not hinder your ability to keep up with your grading. If the problem persists with the same students, try rearranging the seating assignments. Also, remember that if you walk around the room while administering a test, you will automatically discourage a lot of cheating activity.

If the same problem occurs with the same students, schedule a meeting with the parents as the child might have some cheating issues that need to be addressed.

MISTAKE 67:

Letting students do everything as "group" assignments...

Even in elementary school, assigning group work or projects can be a fun way for students to interact and learn. Just be sure to watch the groups and how they function to make sure one or two students are not doing all the work while other students goof off and play.

Some students are natural leaders or so concerned about their grades that they want to take control of the work. These students will naturally enable more relaxed students to not put in their fair share of effort. In early grades, this dynamic might not be so bad. However, as students get older, one of the most common criticisms of advanced students is that they always ended up doing all the work on group projects.

The tendency for smarter students to willingly do all the work while other student's goof off could have something to do with the tendency for gifted students to be introverts. According to studies, about 60 percent of gifted children are introverted compared with 30 percent of the general population. Furthermore, approximately 75 percent of highly gifted children are introverted (Silverman 2014).

While there are certainly advanced students who are extroverts, it is far more likely that you will find introverts among your gifted children. This means that while they are perfectly capable of carrying the load of a group assignment, they do not have the natural leadership and people management skills to make sure all members of their group contribute to the work.

So instead, gifted students will do the work of the group while resenting that other members are goofing off and having fun. After several years of doing this, these students will care enough about their grades in high school to just assume the role of work horse without even asking their classmates for ideas or contributions. This limits the learning experience for all students.

That is not to say that I think you should strike group work off your teaching methodology – though I am certain some introverts would be happy if I did recommend just that. What I am saying is that you should monitor your group work. Walk around the classroom and sit in on the group as they discuss ideas and complete their assignment. When they all look at you wondering if you are going to give them instruction, tell them you are only there to observe and they should proceed. Your quiet presence will ensure that for at least part of the time, all members of the group are paying attention.

As a college professor teaching nearly 50 students at a time, assigning "group" work and/or discussion might have seemed foolish, but I believed students could learn a lot from each other and that college is a place to see things from other world views. Therefore, when I assigned my students group work, I did just as I recommended above and sat in on each group.

Additionally, I asked them to "grade" each other's contributions to the group and factored those scores into their grades. Surprisingly, they tended to grade each other pretty well. I suppose they could have done this regardless of the amount of work each participant performed, but at least I provided them an outlet to express their opinion of their teammates work. I do not necessarily recommend that for very young students, but it is something that you could try with fifth or sixth grade children.

MISTAKE 68:

Handling plagiarism...

Plagiarism becomes more and more of an issue as you teacher older students. It can take on a couple of different forms – your student can copy work word for word, your student can have someone else write the paper, or your student can simply forget to use proper  citation in their paper. Each possibility comes with different issues to address and the appropriate punishment would probably vary.

First, if you are teaching older students and plan to assign research papers as part of your curriculum, you should have a plagiarism policy and make sure you spend ample time teaching your children how to properly cite their references. If you find that your student has merely failed to use proper citations, you should grade them accordingly but not fail their total effort.

If a student copies information word for word without using proper quotation or citing their reference, you should talk to them about plagiarism and citation and give them an opportunity to correct their effort. While a student will not have this opportunity when they are older, it is reasonable to use this as a learning opportunity at this age.

The ability of high school and college students to purchase papers online is abundant. I know more than one person who earned extra money this way in college. However, this is considered cheating for both the person doing the writing and the person claiming the work as their own. If you believe your students have had a little too much help from a friend or their parents, talk to them about their effort. If during that conversation, you come to believe the student needs to put more personal work into their paper, give them the chance to write it again with a small grade penalty.

Again, I realize that students will not have these opportunities in middle and high school, but providing them the chance to complete honest work and still receive a grade will hopefully encourage them to do the work themselves in the future.

CHAPTER 8:
Projects & Reports

Poster boards, book reports, presentations, and other projects are a great way to engage a student in learning and teach them several important skills. They are also bound to irritate the heck out of many parents and frustrate others to the edge of reason. Will you assign them? Of course, and your more experienced co-workers who are parents themselves will as well. Will parents resent and perhaps even hate you for it? Probably.

While I realize that anyone can get into teaching at any point in their lives, if you are a recent, 22ish graduate with your degree freshly framed, I understand that you may not yet be a parent. And if you are, your child is probably not in school yet. Therefore, you have not had the delightful experience of helping your child complete one of the many creative learning projects you will assign.

My personal recommendation is that you borrow a niece or nephew, best friend's child, or neighborhood kid and give these assignments a "test drive" yourself before you roll them out to your classroom. But if that is not a reasonable possibility and you still want to try to keep parents in your corner, pay heed to the recommendations in this chapter on things to avoid.

MISTAKE 69:

Getting overly creative with book reports...

Teaching children a love of reading is possibly one of the most important things you can do as a teacher. If a child falls in love with reading, they will have whole worlds open to them the rest of their lives. And I certainly understand that beyond teaching children to love reading, you must also evaluate how well they are reading and comprehending what they've read.

A book report seems like an effective way to evaluate a student's progress in this regard. Of course, a book report's complexity should be based on the age of the student. You will expect less of younger children than older ones. And you might think that making things a little "fun" will make the whole experience of giving a book report more enjoyable for your students. While you could be correct, be sure that you are not making things overly complicated for the parents.

Plenty of studies show the benefits of engaged parents. But now it seems like teachers operate as if they are assigning work to parents as well as the students. I fail to see why this is a valid teaching practice. Your student is the child in your classroom, not their parent. The parent has already gone through elementary school and now – hopefully – has a job, a house to take care of, and family to look after. In my opinion, any assignment given a child should be something they can complete with minimal supervision from parents.

How do you know if the child could complete the assignment without parental involvement? Ask yourself if the children could do the project in your classroom while you monitor their work. If the answer is no, simplify the project. Of course, this recommendation applies to more than just book reports; it applies to any special assignment you give to your students.

On the specific issue of book reports, what you really need to do is make sure the students can communicate the important parts of the book such as title, author, key characters, significant plot points, and conclusion. Having your students create posters boards with pictures to illustrate some of those key elements could prove fun for the children. But anything more complex could just end up making the parents feel like they should have read the book instead as they try to help their child complete the assignment.

MISTAKE 70:

Assigning "art" projects for core subjects...

You are teaching your students about the Seven Wonders of the Ancient World, so what could be more fun for your students – and their parents – than a project to make a model of one of the "wonders" out of popsicle sticks and cotton balls! Do not expect much on Teacher Appreciation Day if you try something like this early in the year.

While there are many studies promoting the importance of art in the education of children, not all children enjoy it or are good at it. For them, an assignment like the one I just described would be pure torture. If you make it a "test" grade for a subject like history, then you just put what might be an otherwise really good history student at a serious disadvantage. When assessing how well students are learning a subject such as history or science, grading them for their artistic abilities is inappropriate.

In addition to an "art" project not being a good way to measure how well a student is mastering history or science, my recommendation about not assigning projects that children cannot complete on their own still stands. Making parents pull their hair out trying to come up with a design scheme for recreating the Hanging Gardens of Babylon out of foam is not the best way to endear yourself to them. Hand this type of assignment out right before winter or spring break and you might actually get some angry letters.

Again, if you cannot picture supervising your students doing the assignment in your classroom, do not send it home for the parents to endure. Also, if you assign a project that requires more than a quick stop by the Dollar Store, rethink the assignment. You should not send children home with a set of instructions that requires parents to stop by the hardware store. Keep things simple for yourself, the parents, and the students.

MISTAKE 71:

Not expecting parents to do at least half the work...

If you do not heed either of the previous recommendations and proceed to assign your students a project that will undoubtedly require their parents to get involved, do not "grade down" if it appears parents have done "too much" of the work.

Once parents have to begrudgingly get involved in this type of school project, it is a bit unfair to penalize the student for needing that help. And I admit that not all parents hate this type of thing. Some actually enjoy these artsy projects and cannot wait to sit around and help their children create the most beautiful replica of the Tower of London the third grade class at Washington Grover Elementary has ever seen. The other parents hate those moms and dads only slightly more than they hate teachers who give these assignments.

However, almost all parents understand that if they leave their children to their own devices they will most likely fail to meet your requirements and not do well on the project. Therefore, parents will get involved and will probably do at least half of the work, if not more. Most likely, you will be able to tell if certain students had help but you will be unsure about others. It would be unfair to take points off some projects without knowing for certain that the other students did not have help.

As a result, these projects should probably involve research and be graded solely on the basis of whether or not the students follow the instructions.

MISTAKE 72:

Assigning science projects that are just reports...

Once a child reaches middle school or high school, a science project takes on a certain meaning. They generally involve a hypothesis that can be tested, measurable results, and a conclusion. Therefore, a science project is not a report about bees.

It is certainly acceptable to have elementary-aged children do poster boards about a subject that you want them to research. In the area of science, this can be an interesting way for them to learn facts about animals, weather, plants, etc., but calling these science projects leaves the wrong impression on the children and can even confuse them later when it comes time to learn about the scientific method.

Again, if you decide to assign a science poster, try to make it something that the student can research and assemble relatively easily. Otherwise, the parents of your students will learn a great deal about bees, but the students may retain very little. Furthermore, if you have the students do some of the research in your school library, you can make sure they are learning how to do research while putting less pressure on the parents.

CHAPTER 9:
Student Nightmares

Almost everyone has something – perhaps more than one something – from their school years that they were forced to do that they absolutely hated. For some students, it might have been bad enough to elicit a small panic attacks. As a teacher, you should know that there are some things you will need to "force" your students to do and other things you can give them a break on.

While public speaking is a skill that students need to form some basic, rudimentary ability in, not every child is going to grow up to give mass speeches on a daily basis. As a result, a student might need to deliver a short presentation in front of the class at one point or another, but you do not need to repeatedly call on a quiet child in an effort to involve them.

There are many ways to assess whether or not a child is mastering the material you are teaching. And ultimately, you are not grading a child on how well they talk in front of the class or how well they do board work – just whether or not they can perform the skills you have taught. If you can sense that an exercise causes a child stress, try to minimize how often you ask them to do it.

MISTAKE 73:

Calling on students at random to answer questions...

You might think this is a good way to see who is paying attention and measure how well your less outgoing students are grasping the material. The problem is that a child might be failing to raise their hand not because they are daydreaming or ignorant of the answer, but because they are uncomfortable speaking in front of the class. I am not suggesting that you only call on children who volunteer 100 percent of the time, but perhaps you do not need to catch a student completely off guard to accomplish your goal.

Try telling the students ahead of time that you will be asking questions of each student in order, starting on one side of the room at the start of the row and continuing back and across until each child has had their chance to participate. Make it clear to the students that if they do not know the answer, all they have to do is say so and there is no reason to be embarrassed.

Leveraging a strategy like this, the student knows a question is coming and what it will likely pertain to. They can also prepare themselves ahead of time to tell you if they do not know the answer, so they do not have to fear your disapproval if that is the case. The student also knows everyone else in the room will be answering questions as well, so at most, they will only be called upon once and then they can relax.

MISTAKE 74:

Forcing children to do boring work...

Brandy Mayer, a self-proclaimed introvert who works as a Clerk of Courts in New Orleans, told me that as a child she hated things that put pressure on her in school. Being forced to do problems on the board was a particularly high negative. "It freaked me out and made me dread classes," she said.

I am not a natural introvert, but I was shy as a child. Yet, I never minded working a problem on the board and it never really occurred to me that some people feared such exercises. But that is the thing about children, you cannot tell what will fill them with fear and what they can easily brush off. Keep this in mind as you engage with your children and if you can tell that one is particularly uncomfortable with an exercise, let them skip it if you can. If you are required to assess students in that manner, minimize the amount of times you have to ask them to do it.

Just remember that children are not likely to tell you bluntly what makes them nervous or uncomfortable so it is up to you to pay attention.

MISTAKE 75:

Making children share something about themselves...

A teacher asking students to tell everyone their name and share something about themselves is about as common a practice as using a No. 2 pencil on a test. However, it is a practice that many people – even as adults – positively hate. By the time students reach high school, they have started rehearsing this little introduction, but when they are young, they likely have no idea what to say.

This practice in school actually translates into what is commonly referred to as the "elevator speech" by the time a person is of the right age to participate in a career search. Therefore, I cannot deny that it is good practice to start preparing children for making these little speeches later in life. However, you may want to provide them with some guidance.

Rather than asking children to tell the class something about themselves and leaving it as a general, open-ended direction, go ahead and give them specific guidance on what information to share. Ask them to talk about their families, favorite color, hobbies, or summer activities. Simply helping the child narrow down their choices can reduce their anxiety over answering this question. And in the worst scenarios, be sure to make it clear that their name is sufficient.

CHAPTER 10:
Subject-Specific Guidelines

There are a host of errors you can make when teaching any one specific subject, but this chapter focuses on a few common ones along with explanations as to why you should avoid them. These are not hard and fast rules, and certainly not all teachers will follow these recommendations, but you might find that if you avoid these tactics, your students will perform remarkably better.

MISTAKE 76:

Not requiring students to show their work on math tests...

The idea of showing work infuriates some people. They insist it just is not necessary and to a certain point, they might be correct. But as children age and math becomes more complex, having a child show their work will help you evaluate what they are doing wrong when they get an answer incorrect. Without work shown, it is almost impossible to pinpoint what the child fails to understand. They might resent showing work at first, but if doing so helps you help them improve their grade, it is worth their annoyance.

MISTAKE 77:

Making children read out loud for reading time...

It is important to have children read out loud as it helps you evaluate how well they read and how well they understand the words in the books. However, if a child has difficulty reading, if they have a slight stutter, or if they have an accent, making them read aloud could make them nervous and associate negative feelings with reading.

Try having your students read just a couple of lines each as a group, so that they do not have to fear long reading passages. If no one seems too nervous during these activities, you can try longer periods. On the other hand, if this seems to work for your class but you want to evaluate student's reading abilities better, try to have them read in small groups, pairs, or to you individually as a classroom exercise. This might take longer to evaluate, but you will probably get a better sense of their capabilities because fear will not negatively impact skill.

MISTAKE 78:

Overemphasizing date memorization in history...

There are many dates in history that are significant, but try to make history lessons about something more than just calendars. Spend significant periods of time on key events and talk about the people involved in the events you are studying. When you ask a question on an exam, combine other key information with the date to trigger the student's memory. For example, instead of just asking "What year did Christopher Columbus discover the New World?" Ask something like, "In 1492, what famous explorer sailed from Europe and discovered the New World?"

MISTAKE 79:

Not teaching children proper safety measures in science...

Science is an area where as students get older, knowing and following proper safety measures is very important. If you are having your children work with microscopes or Bunsen burners or any other such science equipment, make sure they know all the rules for use, storage, and safety.

MISTAKE 80:

Not testing children on spelling rules...

Do not just teach children to memorize their spelling words each week and forget them the next. Teach them and test them on the rules of spelling. If they can understand the rules of spelling, they will become better long-term spellers than if they just remember how a word is spelled. English is complicated in its spelling rules and there are exceptions for every rule you learn. This is a complicated area to teach and you should probably not grade too harshly, but do try to incorporate it into your spelling grade.

MISTAKE 81:

Not working with children on their handwriting...

Many schools across the country no longer require students to learn cursive writing. The general thought process regarding handwriting is that ultimately children will do more typing than anything else in their academic careers. While this may be true, it is still incredibly important that a student's handwriting be legible. You and other teachers need to be able to read their work on tests and homework. If a student's writing is bad enough, they could get marked wrong for material they actually got correct. Do not let a student pass your grade without working to improve bad handwriting.

CHAPTER 11:
Grading

Assuming you are not one of those teachers who takes great pleasure in being impossible to pass or one who feels like they must give a certain amount of C's and D's to be taken seriously, you will likely want to help your students bring their grades up. Let me first say that I do not believe in handing A's out like the professors at Harvard apparently do (where recent studies show rampant grade inflation and an average grade per class of A-) (Stein 2013, Strauss 2013).

However, I do believe that any teacher of young children can strive for their students to get as many A's or B's in as many subjects as possible (without fudging their test scores to accomplish it). With that said, helping struggling students bring up their grades should be a large focus of any teacher. This section is dedicated to advising first-year teachers how to do that in an effective and efficient manner.

MISTAKE 82:

Not grading participation...

Having taught several college courses, I have structured my grading scale in numerous ways. I find that I do not like grading attendance, but I do believe it is important to grade  participation. There are numerous ways to do this when teaching adults, but I believe it is a mistake not to find some way to apply this concept to elementary-aged students as well.

While some students are shy and difficult to draw out of their shells, many are open, full of questions, and more than happy to "participate" in learning activities. Engaging a student in participation activities is a great way to keep their little minds from wandering, prevent them from getting bored, and really help them grasp a lesson.

Since participation is a valid way to learn, you should put some grading emphasis on it. If you plan to make 10 percent of your grade a participation grade and setup activities to evaluate that grade, you are encouraging yourself not to skimp on this aspect of learning.

Additionally, a student who engages in class by creating and presenting a topic on a poster, talking about a book they are reading, or acting out a skit on a segment of history he or she is learning demonstrates some subject mastery. Even if they are not able to translate that understanding of the subject into a perfect test score, they should receive some credit for their work. A minor participation grade not only helps students engage in class, but it can also bolster the confidence of a student who might not test well but is still learning.

MISTAKE 83:

Grading for neatness...

While you are working on teaching students neatness, they will be developing their small motor skills at different rates. Many children enjoy drawing and coloring very much, and others do not enjoy these exercises at all. If a student is developmentally delayed in terms of small motor skills, they might realize that their coloring or drawing skills leave something to be desired. In fact, they might not enjoy this activity simply because they know they are bad at it. As a result, coloring or drawing something they know they will be graded on might cause them a great amount of anxiety.

Therefore, when you assign a coloring or drawing exercise, be sure to let the students know they should do the best they can at being neat, but you will be grading for factual accurateness or for "correctness." In this manner, your non-artists will not become worried about having their grades hurt when they otherwise know the material but just cannot color or draw well.

MISTAKE 84:

Not grading for neatness at all...

Conversely, there are times when students need to learn to achieve a certain amount of neatness. If you cannot read their handwriting at all or they write their numbers and letters without paying attention to the lines on their paper, you might need to take some points off in order to get them to try harder in this area.

The simple fact is that if students cannot learn to write coherently, they will be marked wrong on tests and homework assignments where they may actually be correct. If you can help them achieve a level of neatness in their writing that is legible, this will benefit them in all of their future academic pursuits. So while you do not need to be punitive in your grading for students who cannot color, you might need to consider taking off points for students who are extremely amiss in their writing abilities – particularly if you are confident if they take their time, they can do a better job.

When to award or take off points for neatness might very well end up being a judgment call on your part, but you should probably work into your grading system some kind of policy you can communicate to your students and apply it evenly across the board.

MISTAKE 85:

Not giving extra credit...

I am a big believer in extra credit. I feel if a student is on the cusp of a higher grade and they want to put in some extra work to bring it up, they should be given the opportunity to do so. I think extra credit is a good practice to begin even with elementary-aged students.

Personally, I would advise that you plan it into your tests and curriculum. Provide bonus questions on tests and assign extra credit sheets for every nine weeks. However, if you do not plan on giving extra credit but your students ask about it, be quick to accommodate it.

It does not take a lot of extra work to give your students an extra credit assignment, even if you plan it at the last minute. The extra grading might be a little inconvenient as nine weeks or the semester winds down, but not all of your students will do extra credit, so the additional work for you will not be that significant.

I have heard teachers say that "only the good students" do extra credit work or "only the students who do not need it, do the extra credit." These teachers believe that practice is a waste of their time. Having taught hundreds of adults, I can assure you that the extra credit I've given has made a difference for many of my students.

Teaching children at an early age that a little extra work can make a difference to their grade if they do not master the material completely is a valuable lesson in my opinion. Additionally, I think working on extra credit helps students realize that the teacher does care about their grades and is willing to put in a little extra effort to let them improve.

As many of you first-year teachers can probably recall, being able to talk to your professors in college makes a difference in academic performance. Rewarding children for asking for help or extra work is a good way to develop the confidence to approach teachers that will one day immensely benefit their educational pursuits.

MISTAKE 86:

Not giving all of your students the chance to do extra credit...

Of course, once you decide to allow your students the opportunity to do extra credit, you need to extend that offer to all of your students, not just those who ask for it and not just those who need it. While you might be able to identify the students it will help and those it will not make a difference for – to avoid any accusations of favoritism or unfairness, offer extra credit opportunities to your whole class.

MISTAKE 87:

Not offering before- or after-school help...

I know teachers put in long days and, as a first-year teacher, you need to avoid getting overwhelmed and burned out. Perhaps the thought of offering before- or after-school help sessions just does not appeal to you at all. Maybe you think you need that time to take care of other matters so it is possible for you to go home and not have a mile-high pile of things to do at home.

I am not suggesting that you offer these little help sessions every day; I am merely suggesting that once or twice a week you should offer students the opportunity to meet with you to go over work they are struggling with in the class. Your school might offer free tutoring for students, but that is likely to be generic tutoring designed for passing standardized tests. The help sessions you could offer would be more in line with the lessons you are teaching and more beneficial to your students.

In order to avoid getting too stressed out or burdened by before- and after-school help sessions, you can structure that help time to cover certain subjects on specific days and ask students to sign up for the help sessions so you know how many children to expect. I have also seen teachers have a policy that they will only offer help sessions to students with grades of C or below. This will help ensure your time is spent with students who need your help the most.

Offering help sessions like this before and after school and making sure parents are aware of this option can also go a long way to defusing any animosity toward you if a child ends up not doing well in class. So I highly recommend finding a schedule that works for you and adding this into your weekly routine early on in the first nine weeks.

MISTAKE 88:

Not leveraging a student's strengths to help them with their weak areas...

I believe that you can help a student improve by using what they excel in to help increase their understanding and performance in areas where they are weak. For example, if you have students who enjoy coloring and drawing, use their creative and visual talent to draw pictures of the lessons you are teaching. If you have students who are talented writers, readers, or storytellers – try to tie those skills into their math lessons.

The reason for this recommendation is simple; everyone is good at something and using that "something" to help make other subjects make more sense can prove to be an excellent teaching tool. Do not be afraid to use a wide-range of teaching methods to communicate your subject matter and if something is not working, do not be afraid to change your strategy to something that works better for your classroom.

Try to remember that you designed your class material for students you did not know – for nameless, faceless students whose strengths and weaknesses you were blissfully unaware of. Now you know these children and you know what their interests are and what they do well, so now you can customize your existing lesson plans around these individuals you have the privilege of teaching. Be flexible and use strength to promote more strength.

MISTAKE 89:

Not calling the parents soon enough...

In a separate section of this book, I discuss how important the parent partnership is for you in your teaching efforts. This is as true when it comes to academics as when it comes to classroom discipline. Open and frequent communications with parents will allow them to keep their children on track and correct academic slips before they become too severe.

I recommend that, on top of progress reports at the mid-way point in a nine-week grading period (which most teachers provide), that you should also make sure parents are aware of their child's grades on a weekly basis. I have seen teachers achieve them by sending home test packets for parents to sign or a weekly communications log for parents to initial. Using any idea to keep an open dialogue (even through notes) between you and the parents is a good idea.

Leveraging this weekly, open dialogue between you and the parents will help you make them aware of a poor grade or series of poor grades so they can take action before a progress report or report card is issued. Most parents will be grateful for such opportunities because they will want to correct their child's issues or decline before it becomes more serious or too late to address.

In addition to these forms of communications, if you are really concerned about a child's academics, I would recommend that you set up a conference sooner than later. Again, the earlier the parent is aware of negative academic performance, the sooner he/she can help correct it – whether that is making sure the child attends your help sessions, getting the child external tutoring, or helping the child himself/herself.

MISTAKE 90:

Not giving the student the grade they earned...

No matter how hard a child tries, sometimes their grades will not reflect their effort. And yet, "A for Effort" should not be part of your thinking. If you have done your job throughout the school year, working to identify tests you need to curve, assignments you might need to drop since no one did well on them, providing opportunities for extra credit, etc., then you have to give your students the grades they earn.

When you are looking at the final grades, there is no telling what exactly is going to bother you. It may be a student that you know tried real hard, but still ended up with a C. It could be a child that is otherwise a straight A student, but makes a C in math. It could be a student that you have to fail in a subject area because no matter how hard you both worked at it this year, little Jimmie or Suzie just could not grasp the material at grade level. Do not be tempted to "pad" grades if you feel bad for a child. You need to be able to justify those grades and show that you are being fair across the board. Whatever rules you apply to one student, you must apply to all.

MISTAKE 91:

Being unwilling to hold a child back...

In a previous section, I discussed at length the mistake of not using a curve when testing. However, there is a difference between curving a grade on a test or tests and padding students' grades to pass them when they would otherwise fail.

Our education system is rampant with the idea that failure will hurt a child, injure their self-confidence, and apparently make future success nearly impossible. The pressure is so strong to pass children that many students get promoted without learning the necessary skills to advance. This ultimately leads to a portion of the population graduating while functionally illiterate or even worse, students who are allowed to walk on graduation day but are not receiving diplomas – just certificates of attendance.

In the attempt to not ever make a child feel like a failure, you can often fail to give them what they need – an education. Children should not be taught that failure is the worst thing that can happen to them. Instead, they should be taught that not learning from their failure is the worst thing that can happen.

As a teacher, advancing a student who is not prepared is a mistake. Now, I am not talking about a student who is excelling in all subject areas except for one. That student should be able to catch up and keep up with the demands of the next grade level adequately enough. I am talking about a student who has not mastered enough of the material to pass your class.

The plain simple truth is sometimes you have to fail a student, give an F, or hold a child back. It can turn out to be the best thing to happen to the child. They get another year to learn and understand the material and when they do advance they can confidently face their next school year. A failing student can become a good one with another year of practice under their belt.

Conversely, passing a student when he or she is not prepared to face the next school year can do more to erode their self-confidence and make them feel stupid than holding them back would have done. While they might get to stay in the same class as all of their friends, they will continue to struggle, make bad grades, and feel inadequate to the tasks that are put before them.

I am certain that as a first-year teacher, the last thing you want to do is fail a student. You might even wonder if that student's failure is your fault. Do not let your insecurity prevent you from doing the right thing for a student. If you have offered help and extra credit and worked one-on-one with the student, then you should be able to judge if they are ready for the following school year. If you feel they are not, then do them the favor of holding them back.

MISTAKE 92:

Not keeping track of grades well...

One of your most important jobs as a teacher is to evaluate your student's performance and document the results. The subsequent results must be recorded accurately and completely in order to make up the student's final grades. Your school might have a method of recording grades they expect you to use, but you still need to be sure you are organized and methodical in your approach. You do not want to send home graded papers with students before you record them in your grade log. Keeping track of your grades effectively will help you greatly if any student – or more likely parent – challenges your grades at the end of the year. Failing to have a good system could leave you in a lurch.

MISTAKE 93:

Not frequently communicating grades to students/parents...

Believe it or not, there are parents who are anxiously awaiting their children's grades. They spend time studying with their children for big tests and they want to know how their child did. Once a child brings home a less than acceptable grade, the parent might be monitoring their performance to decide what kind of privileges the child has on weekends. Your delay in grading tests and papers and getting that information back to parents could get some of your students in trouble. Make sure you are communicating well with parents and not leaving students desperate trying to make their parents believe that you really did not give the test grades back yet.

CHAPTER 12:
Managing Distractions

From kindergarten to sixth grade, many things can distract children from succeeding. If you thought that all you would have to do is instruct students on math, science, history, and language, then someone lied to you. You will have the privilege of wearing almost as many hats as a mother.

You will, at times, have to deal with personality conflicts among your students, be watchful and prevent bullying, and support children who are friendless. You will also need to ensure a child is not mocked or teased for being poor. Finally, you will need to prevent anything in your classroom from becoming a popularity contest. This is quite a lot of social maneuvering for a teacher to pull off while trying to communicate the day's lesson. But if you do not fulfill these duties, then some students will get left behind academically.

You are probably thinking, "I did not become a teacher to be a social director or a matchmaker or any other such nonsense." Of course, you are correct in this regard, but if you are unwilling to dedicate some of your time to monitoring the distractions that come from how your students relate to one another, you might not be able to maintain the order and structure your students need to thrive. Bullying, teasing, and other petty relationship problems do not just stay on the playground or in the lunchroom – they impact your classroom as well. Be alert.

In addition to distractions that can occur in how students relate to one another, you may have to deal with traditional distractions such as toys and high-tech devices such as phones, tablets, and game systems. While it astonishes me that parents would allow elementary-aged children to have phones and/or not prevent the children from taking game systems to school, this does happen.

If you are a recent graduate from college, then you will likely come from a world where you carry a smart phone and/or tablet on you at all times. You probably used it during your college classes and thought nothing of it – perhaps you even had a cell phone in your backpack in high school. Students having high-tech devices might not even faze you. But I can assure you that if your school has a policy regarding these devices, you should enforce it strictly. If you do not, then you should make a classroom policy for yourself and not waver from it.

Your classroom is not a place for smart phones or tablets – not even in a child's backpack. The last thing you need is to be in a fight between children or parents regarding a costly stolen or damaged item. Below are stories, advice and recommendations regarding dealing with distractions in the classroom.

Best Friends Forever and Worst Enemies

Greeting cards and television commercials show you how cute it is when a little girl decides that a little boy is going to be her boyfriend. What these mediums fail to do is talk about the results of such "relationships" coming to an end. Tears, teasing, and fighting are hardly something you want to spill over into your classroom. While you cannot prevent such things from happening, you can make it clear to your students that whether they like or hate each other, they will respect each other and treat each other with kindness in your classroom.

Respect is an important concept to teach young children and goes way beyond being polite or having manners. Treating others with respect means not going through each other's stuff, not talking behind each other's back, and not teasing each other about what they are wearing or for answering a question wrong in class. It is important that you lead by example because your students will take their cues from you. Below are a few ways to avoid having "best friends" and "worst enemies" disrupt your classroom.

MISTAKE 94:

Letting popularity matter in the classroom...

I cannot emphasize enough how much you should avoid letting popularity become a factor in your classroom. Allowing students to learn and practice the concept of voting is admirable, but I do not feel like young students can vote on a representative with any practical reasoning. Therefore, voting on something like a "class president" or even "best project" could turn into a popularity contest.

Instead, if you want to teach concepts of voting and majority rule, allow your children the choice between two options and let the class vote to select one over the other. This can be a vote on which book to read or craft to work on. As long as you are allowing children to vote between two possibilities, but not two people, you are limiting the popularity contest between individual students.

As you limit these instances for students, keep in mind that you should not show favoritism yourself – not to the students or parents of your students. Furthermore, you should not seek your own popularity in the school or with the students. When you become overly concerned about how well you are liked by students or staff in comparison to other teachers, you will hinder your work.

MISTAKE 95:

Permitting "innocent" teasing...

Most schools proclaim loudly and frequently that they have a "zero-tolerance" policy when it comes to bullying. You are probably ready to address bullying whenever and wherever you see it. Yet, there is teasing that might not qualify as bullying but still should not be permitted in your classroom. You might even have to find yourself making sure you do not engage in it.

Children are often sensitive about things that make them stand out. While you might have a few students whose parents have successfully taught them to love the things about themselves that make them unique, you will have many more students who are sensitive about silly things like having freckles, wearing glasses, or needing braces. You need to ensure that you do not overlook teasing about these little things just because they seem trivial to you.

Many teachers have wet wipes, hand sanitizer, and other such items in their classrooms regularly these days. You might want to also consider having things like deodorant or mouthwash on hand. Remaining fully stocked with these supplies will help you pull some students aside who might need to wash up a bit or deal with bad breath to help them not be embarrassed in front of their classmates. This is a difficult issue to address, and you will need to find a way to do it that will not humiliate the child, but letting students know you have these things available for them could help a student overcome needless teasing.

Other areas where you feel teasing might be "innocent" could come from students snickering about an answer a student gives in class or students teasing a child about liking something other students think is "stupid" or "childish." While these may not be full-blown examples of bullying, you should encourage students to feel comfortable answering questions in your classroom. It can just take one wrong response for a student to clam up and not want to talk anymore. So, while there are "stupid" answers, do not ever let a student feel like he or she gave one. Find something in his or her answer that you can use to move them in the right direction of the lesson and silence students who start to laugh or tease a student for giving a wrong answer quickly.

When it comes to likes and dislikes, children advance through different stages at different ages. You might have a seven-year-old who still likes Thomas the Train and one who is already into super heroes. You should not allow your student to make their classmates feel childish or wrong because of their natural likes or dislikes. This may come up as part of class discussion or aside from it. Encourage your students to be respectful of each other, and this will help you maintain a classroom where each child feels free to express themselves and participate in your learning exercises.

MISTAKE 96:

Letting fights or bickering impact the classroom...

One of the things that's been most surprising for me raising a daughter is how early girls can get into "cat fights." I simply do not recall such problems when I was young. Of course, boys can get into playground scuffles and  have their own version of "cattiness" as well. While this is going to happen in school, you must do what you can to prevent it from carrying over into your classroom.

It is fine if two or more of your students are upset with each other as long as they do not express it while you are teaching a lesson. If you need to separate students, then do so. I do not think you need to keep young children in their assigned seating and expect them to behave when ill feelings are forming between them. A little space might just help you keep your classroom under control.

Of course, if students make faces at one another and try to rile each other up every time you turn around, you might need to send them to the principal's office. If that happens, make sure you send both students so the issue can be dealt with fairly. Go ahead and admit to yourself that there are things you might have missed so that even if one child appears to be the instigator and another the victim, the principal probably needs to hear both sides of the story.

The important thing is that you do not allow a temporary or even long-lasting fight or disagreement between two or more of your students to have an impact on your classroom. Ensuring students understand that they need to respect each other and get along, or there will be negative consequences for all involved, is one way to motivate students to make the extra effort to settle down for you.

MISTAKE 97:

Trying to settle a student squabble or restore a broken friendship...

While you need to make sure an argument does not get out of hand (and you can lecture both students on issues such as respect and kindness), you should not attempt to solve the fight itself. Children who hate each other one week will once again be best friends the next, and they will do this on their own without any adult intervention. Your job is to ensure that your classroom is not negatively impacted while these pendulum swings occur.

In most cases, you will not need to listen to detailed stories about why one child no longer likes another. You might need to intervene if a child messed with another child's property, but you do not have to be a relationship counselor to seven-year-olds. They can often work it out on their own. Intervening any more than necessary to maintain a healthy learning environment could exaggerate how much of a distraction the squabbling proves to be – both for you and the students.

MISTAKE 98:

Taking sides...

Do not ever take sides – even if you really want to, even if you believe one child is completely right and another is completely wrong. When children come to you with a problem, listen to them and consult with your supervisor or the school principal on how to handle the situation. If you immediately appear to take a side in the situation, you can be accused of bias or favoritism. In order to successfully resolve conflict, you must avoid such appearances.

Enlisting a third party to help resolve conflict between students in your classroom is probably the best way to go. While you could serve as an arbitrator between your students, and since you need to maintain classroom order, having one or both of them think you are unfair and favored the other student will not help you. Instead, seek help and support from the staff around you and make your main focus maintaining classroom order, not telling the children which one of them is right and which one is wrong.

MISTAKE 99:

Not recognizing and stopping bullying...

Every time you hear an adult talk about how they were bullied as a child, it seems like that behavior was so blatant that some adult – some teacher – should've observed the behavior and done something about it. It is almost impossible to believe that bullying behavior always exists in a bubble where surrounding adults remain blissfully unaware. Yet it is equally difficult to imagine an adult witnessing bullying and doing nothing about it.

The lesson you need to take from this is to be observant of children in the halls, lunchrooms, and as they get on and off buses. Do not just watch your students in your classroom: watch them everywhere. You could be teaching first graders and see nothing amiss, but your students might be being bullied by fourth graders when they go to the bathroom.

At this age, children should still be a little intimidated by all adults. If you see bullying, handle it according to your school's policy. Do not turn around and walk the other way or think some other teacher will handle it. There are things you can stay out of – like school politics – as a new teacher, but not wanting to be confrontational when one child is bullying another is not a luxury you have at any time in your career.

High and Low-Tech Distractions

As much as student interactions with each other can cause children to be distracted from the learning process, inanimate objects can cause the same problems. This section will address things that are as simple as a toy ring to something as complicated as a smart phone or tablet. You should understand your school's policy on such issues and be prepared to enforce it. However, if your school is lax in this area, you might want to develop a stricter policy yourself, communicate it to all students and parents, and be prepared to back it up.

Technology and toys are great developments. You can use low- and high-tech devices to engage your children in the learning process. But this practice should be in your control and under your supervision. Anything that falls outside of those parameters is more likely to cause problems than to advance the learning process.

MISTAKE 100:

Not having a policy about toys or other items from home...

First and foremost, you need to have a classroom policy regarding toys and other items from home. If you are not going to permit any toys to come to class, then you need to communicate that to both parents and children. This means you might have to confiscate toys from children and return them at the end of the day to be taken home. It might mean you have to confiscate toys until the parents themselves can come pick them up.

If such policies seems harsh to you or a recipe for having parents upset with you, remember that children are extremely bad at mixing up their belongings. Would you rather confiscate a toy, mark who it belongs to, and put it in your desk? Or have two students claim the same doll belongs to them and have no way of determining who owns the doll? Which scenario is more likely to lead to an upset parent?

Should you decide to permit children to bring certain items and toys from home for "show and tell" or to be played with during classroom "down time," be sure to implement a strong labeling system. As I mentioned before, children can mix up their toys, or worse, trade toys, much to their parents' dismay. While you might want to say that any jewelry or toys or books that a child brings from home is the child's and the parent's responsibility, that will not save you from upset parents blaming you if things go wrong. "No take-backs" is not as amusing in real life as it is on television sitcoms.

Whatever you decide, be sure you have firm policies that will help you prevent arguments among your students and anger from their parents.

MISTAKE 101:

Not confiscating toys...

As an extension of the previous mistake, not being willing to confiscate a toy or device at all is a terrible mistake. Telling the child to put the toy or device away might  solve the problem, but there are times when you are going to have to resolve a situation by taking something away from a student.

It is better that you determine how to do this and communicate the process ahead of time to your students. That way, you can prevent the child from becoming angry or even scared that you are not going to return the item to them later. If you do not have a policy in place, then what was a distraction might turn your classroom upside down if the child overreacts.

Not being willing to take a toy away in order to avoid such a reaction is not a good policy either. There are going to be times when it is necessary to confiscate something. Be prepared for it to happen, and you will avoid headaches in the future.

MISTAKE 102:

Allowing phones and other devices in your classroom...

My personal opinion regarding phones and high-tech devices is that elementary-aged children do not need them and should not bring them to your class. Your school might have a similar policy. If that's the case, just enforce the school's rules. If you are allowed some leniency, you will need to decide how much responsibility you are willing to shoulder in your classroom if you permit such devices.

There are a few things I believe you should consider if you decide to allow phones and high-tech devices in your classroom. First is the cost of such items if they are lost or damaged. You might consider this solely the responsibility of the parent and child, but you could well be put in the situation where a parent expects to hold you accountable for stolen or damaged property. Regardless of how such an issue is resolved, it puts you in a situation that would be uncomfortable at any point in your teaching career, let alone your first year.

Another thing to consider is how secure are your student's possessions in your classroom. While lockers are more common in middle school and high school, if you have them, then you might feel safer allowing these devices than if you only had cubby holes for the children to put their stuff in. You might also want to consider if the school provides the lock to the locker or if the child bought it. In other words, how easy would it be for someone to break into the locker or get the combination from someone other than the student. All of these factors determine how responsible it is for a student to expect something they bring from home will be safe.

Finally, you should consider what the benefit of having the device is versus the potential negative that could come from having it in your classroom.

If the cost outweighs the benefit, adopt a policy accordingly. If you feel the benefit is worth a little bit of risk, adopt a policy that accounts for and seeks to minimize risk as much as possible and proceed from that point.

MISTAKE 103:

Rewarding students with treats at the wrong time of day...

While many teachers would not allow children to bring a toy from home, they are big believers in rewards of "treasure boxes." Certainly these "carrots" can be an excellent way to encourage children to do well in both behavior and grades, but be careful not to award these treats in the middle of the day.

There is something to be said for a student being immediately rewarded for positive behavior. It makes a strong connection that reinforces the positive achievement. However, you do not need to accomplish this with an immediate trip to the treasure box or instant reward. Giving the student a receipt that they will receive the reward at the end of the day or even at the end of the week should be sufficient for reinforcing the positive behavior. That way, there is immediate positive reinforcement without a toy or treat becoming a distraction in your classroom.

Also, remember that reward time will turn the students' attention away from whatever you are trying to communicate and onto the reward itself. Therefore, do not try to use an instant reward while teaching a lesson or reviewing for a test. Keep the children focused on the task at hand with the promise of the reward to follow at a planned time when you do not need your students' full attention.

Additionally, if you provide behavioral or academic rewards early in the day, you might diminish a child's motivation to perform well the rest of the day. They could feel as if they have achieved the desired result already and can relax. In order to keep children motivated until you are ready for them to relax, plan your treasure and treat time accordingly.

MISTAKE 104:

Not making your policy clear to parents, and not asking for their help in enforcing your rules...

Pretty much any rule you make for your classroom needs to be understood and acknowledged by the parents of your students. This is particularly true when it comes to toys and devices. Whatever your policy is, parents need to understand and become an active participant in reinforcing it on their end.

More importantly though, you need parents to be aware of your policy so that if you have to enforce a punishment, then they will not be upset or angry with you. If your policy is that a parent needs to come pick up any toy or device that is confiscated, that is something they need to know well in advance so it does not come as a surprise when it happens.

There is nothing wrong with having strict classroom rules. You just need to make sure parents are aware of these rules so they become your partner in the process. As always with parents, active communication is the key to building successful relationships.

Classroom Emergencies

The distractions that come from classroom "emergencies" can run the gamut from potty breaks to fire drills to bomb threats. In some cases, you can manage the emergency so that it does not distract too heavily from your class. In the more serious instances, you can only manage the emergency well and maintain order while you lead your students through the situation. No matter what the nature of the emergency might be, there are a number of mistakes you should avoid – read on to learn more.

MISTAKE 105:

Having too strict of a bathroom policy...

One issue that the teachers of elementary-aged children face is how to know when a child really needs to go to the bathroom. As amusing as this dilemma seems now, it is amazing how something as small as a "bathroom break" can interrupt your classroom in a major way. It starts with one little hand in the air asking to go potty and turns into a sequence of children lining up to use the bathroom whether they really need to or not.

In order to avoid such potty outbreaks, you might create a bathroom plan for your classroom that involves specific times when children can go use the restroom. However, if you do so, be prepared to make exceptions.

Children may, at times, need to use the bathroom more frequently than normal. If they do not typically ask to use the bathroom at unusual times, you probably want to err on the side of caution and let them go.

Ultimately, as much as you need to minimize interruptions to your classroom, having a potty accident will be more disruptive than letting the child have the bathroom pass.

MISTAKE 106:

Not helping students cover up a mishap...

In the book "25 Biggest Mistakes Teachers Make" by Carolyn Orange, she shares the story of a person who in first grade had an accident in class during naptime. Rather than help the student deal with the accident without other children noticing, the teacher made the child clean up the mess and go out the front door with a wastebasket full of soiled paper towels and head to the principal's office (Orange 2007).

If something like this happens in your classroom, there is really no reason not to try to minimize the child's embarrassment. You should let the child get to the office so they can call their parents while you do something to distract the class and clean up the mess. While it will probably be difficult to have the whole incident pass unnoticed by the other children, downplay what happened as much as possible so the child is not made fun of for months to come.

MISTAKE 107:

Not dealing with a child's vomiting in a professional manner...

The sight and sound of a person vomiting is enough to make me gag, so I do not envy the teacher who has to handle a child getting sick to their stomach at school. However, it is important that you deal with such accidents without freaking out.

If a student approaches you about having an upset stomach, you should send them to the bathroom first and then to the school nurse/office. As you get to know your students better as the year progresses, you will be able to tell which child gets butterflies before a test and which student is likely to vomit if they say they do not feel well. Until such time, be on the side of caution and save yourself the clean up.

MISTAKE 108:

Not knowing exactly what to do in case of a fire drill, bomb threats, etc...

Whether your school is having a routine fire drill or an unexpected tornado warning or bomb threat, you need to know exactly what your students need to do in all situations. Your children will look to you in all situations and you do not want your experience with a routine fire drill to look like an early scene from the movie, "Kindergarten Cop."

Familiarize yourself with all of your school's standard operating procedures when it comes to emergency situations, know where to take your children, and communicate to your children what they need to do in each instance.

Boredom

Perhaps there is little more distracting to a child than being bored. There are up and down sides to living in the age of the internet. It seems like children are more accustomed to being electronically stimulated than ever before. Therefore, having to sit still while waiting for classmates to finish an assignment or test could be enough to make a child fidget or misbehave.

Your job is not to constantly entertain your students, but you should try to minimize the possible negative impact boredom can have on your classroom. However, in doing this, I caution you to be aware of how you could deemphasize the importance of a test in the process. Read on, for examples of mistakes to avoid when combating boredom.

MISTAKE 109:

Assigning too much work...

In researching this book, I came across the concept that you should not allow children to sit around with nothing important to do at any point in time. I realize that this seems like good advice since you have a lot of material to cover and you need to make sure your students grasp it all before the year is through. But there is such a thing as information overload.

In most schools across the country, children are getting less and less playtime outside. There is a ton of research that validates that outside play and exercise benefit the learning process, but schools just do not have time to fit it in anymore. While this may be your problem, there is little you can do to correct it. Instead, you have to work around it.

However, I do not believe the best way to work around children getting bored or fidgety is to just assign more work. First, some children need more time to complete work than others and they should not feel pressure to finish because other students have started on something else. Next, when a student has completed a hard test or assignment, it could be helpful to let them relax for a few minutes and recoup for the next section of the day. Handing them more work robs them of the chance to have some downtime.

Set a reasonable goal for how much work you can get through in a day and allow yourself some room for if the days goes faster or slower than expected. If you find your students need more time on a subject, slow down and go over the material again. If you run through the day quickly, have a learning activity planned that will reinforce what you are teaching but also let the children have a little fun.

Or you can reward the children with a little "free" time while you sit at your desk and do some work. If this scares you, remember that not every minute of a child's day needs to be scheduled. Allowing them some time in the day to study, work ahead on homework, color, or read gives them a little bit of flexibility in an otherwise very structured environment. If the class starts to get unruly, you will need to step in, but you might find that they can handle a little free time and still behave well.

MISTAKE 110:

Not using hands-on work...

You probably do not want to have your students dancing around your classroom all too often, so you may not be able to give them the physical outlet they need on days when they get restless. However, you can be sure to engage them in plenty of hands-on or demonstrative activities. "Once a teacher brought in cupcakes and straws to explain a science concept to us," explained Brandy Mayer. "When she put the straw into the center of the cupcake for a sample, it came out with different layers of filling. I liked it when teachers were creative like that."

You do not need to run out and become a master baker, but using a few hands-on activities to demonstrate science or math principles may help engage your students in a subject they otherwise find boring. Also, try to remember that young children learn very well with their hands. As a result, puzzles or other learning games that involve assembling things can be an effective way for some students to master a lesson.

MISTAKE 111:

Handing out puzzle or coloring sheets after a test...

Giving children something they can do after a test to keep them quiet probably seems like a good idea. Unfortunately, I have observed that children might rush through a test if they become overly aware of the fact that they are lagging behind their classmates.

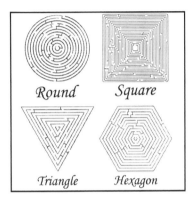

Round   *Square*

Triangle   *Hexagon*

If you have allotted a certain amount of time for these tests, being the first or the last student to turn in the assignment should not matter, but for some reason it does to many children. If they think you are handing out an assignment they are going to have to complete later, that puts even more pressure on them to work faster and finish.

Rather than create the impression that a student needs to hurry along in an exam, have the children read after they finish a test or assignment instead. Reading will keep the children quiet while not signaling to other students that they need to rush. Also, be sure to communicate before the start of a test how long the children will have to complete the work and that you will give them a warning when they are getting close to needing to turn the papers in.

CHAPTER 13:
Overcoming Challenges Your Students Present

As a teacher, you are going to see all kinds of students, which means you are going to have to become familiar with all kinds of learning challenges. Some challenges might be internal to the student (such as having a lack of focus), while others are external factors (such as having a student who doesn't have internet access at home).

You can't fix all of these problems yourself, but you can prepare yourself to help out. If you recognize the challenges affecting a child's work, you can work to help him or her overcome whatever it is he or she might be dealing with.

MISTAKE 112:

Not knowing how to deal with students who have no focus...

This is going to be a problem that you will face at one point or another, and it might even be with multiple students at once. It might be a core issue — an issue that is across the board. For example, you may come across a student that keeps talking when he or she should be working, or that can't keep his or her eyes from wandering around the room during class.

On the other hand, you may come across a student that can't stay focused because he or she just is not interested in the subject or material that you're teaching. Perhaps the way the material is being taught is just not interesting or engaging for someone in his or her age group.

If you have a student that is completely devoid of anything resembling focus, that might be a situation better suited for a guidance counselor, psychologist, or doctor, and you should do your best to set up an initial meeting. However, if your students are experiencing sporadic lacks in focus, there are things you can do.

You need to do your best to make your lessons as engaging and as inspiring as humanly possible. Even if you are teaching your students about how paint dries, it is your duty to catch their interest in one way or another. Think of your target audience. Perhaps you can use multimedia components, interesting and modern examples for outdated history lessons, or even a story to get them interested. Your job as a teacher is to interest your students and make the material relevant.

If you involve your students in one way or another and keep them engaged in the learning process, you are bound to have more success with the students who are struggling to stay focused. Imagine that you are basically tricking your students into learning what you need them to learn. Have fun with it and your students will as well.

MISTAKE 113:

Not knowing how to deal with students who have a busy schedule...

Even young students are getting involved with extracurricular activities these days. While it is not your job to cater to these students, you do need to know how to deal with them when the situation arises.

How you deal with a situation relies heavily on the individual student, but here is an example. Let us say that you have a student involved in basketball, choir, and band. He (or she) has a game, a choir rehearsal, and a band rehearsal all within a two-day period, and these are conveniently on the same days you had your big exam planned.

It can be tempting to offer this student an extension or additional help, but life cannot always cater to the schedule of your students. If you do not let your students learn how to balance their schedules now, you are doing them a disservice. Since they are very young, though, perhaps you may feel that parents are interfering and making their student's life busier than it needs to be. Set up a conference with them to discuss keeping their students priorities straight.

This works the same way if you happen to be one of the few teachers who has students that miss large chunks of school for various reasons — for example, you might have a celebrity student who must leave school to do some type of work. You might think that this would never happen to you, but it has to happen to someone, right?

The rapper Drake, for example, dropped out of high school to act on the hit TV series *Degrassi: The Next Generation*. He made the decision to drop out of school in order to balance his life. This is likely not something that will happen with young students, but you have to remember that different students and their families might have different responsibilities and priorities.

Do your best to keep open lines of communication between you and parents to ensure what's best for the student is what's happening. If a student is falling behind because of too many commitments, make sure parents know that you cannot constantly extend deadlines, change the attendance policy, or give any kind of special treatment to one particular student.

MISTAKE 114:

Expecting students to be as smart as you are...

Youngsters are getting better and better at figuring out technology. But you still need to be careful when assuming what students will know how to use. Since your students are so young, assume nothing when it comes to what a student will know how to do. Don't let a student become embarrassed because he or she doesn't know how to use a certain technology or because his or her family can't afford certain technology.

There is a chance that your students might not have a computer at home, so be careful about assigning homework that requires the internet or use of a printer. Make sure to allow ample time for those students that might need to make arrangements to use the school's computers to get things done.

If you are an experienced teacher you might not have this problem, but be careful about using language that children may not understand because it is far above their grade level. Remember the age group that you are speaking to. Keep things easy to explain and easy to understand so that no one will feel lost in your classroom.

If you think an assignment is too complicated, be sure to provide your students with learning material, such as links to online tutorials or a detailed list of steps. The most important thing as a teacher is that your students are learning something. Do not let them be embarrassed for not being as far along in the learning process as some of their classmates may be.

MISTAKE 115:

Not knowing how to deal with students who struggle with criticism...

Some of your students will really struggle if you try to correct them or tell them they did something wrong. You have to help them learn to deal with being wrong and how to handle it positively. You might feel a bit of a struggle between the desire to effectively teach your students and the desire to protect them from hurt feelings.

Here are some general tips to follow when trying to correct your students' mistakes:

Carefully monitor your body language. When you have to tell a student they did something poorly or got something wrong, it is important to remember that your body language is just as important as your words. If you cross your arms, are towering over them, or have a tense face, the students will pick up on these nonverbal cues and tense up as well. Try to keep your arms comfortably at your sides, do your best to be at eye-level, and give them feedback with a smile.

Give feedback often. If you never give feedback and the first time you do so is to tell the student something really negative, it will be painful regardless of your body language. It is important to make this a regular occurrence so that your students expect it and become accustomed to feedback, good or bad. Your students will be much more receptive when things go wrong if you make this a habit.

Do not over-praise your students. If you praise your students too often for a job well-done, it can actually turn into a negative thing. If there is no variance in your feedback, they won't want to try different things. It can eventually harm their self-esteem if you continue to give the same feedback all the time. Make sure your students know when they're right, when they're wrong, and how to keep learning.

Do not leave students high and dry. Make sure that if you have to say something negative to your students that you help them figure out what's next. Don't drop bad news on a student and then leave them to deal with it on their own. Work together to come up with new plans for improvement. Set some goals that they can achieve so that they will remain positive and inspired.

Ask your students questions. "What can you do differently to solve this problem?" or "How can we make this assignment go from a good one to a great one?"

Know what to expect. If you have to use criticism, make sure it is constructive. Students will either get defensive or completely shut down when experiencing criticism. Make each lesson a positive one. Teach them to separate the criticism of their work from criticism of them as a person. They need to understand you are not attacking them personally.

This can make teaching really tough, but you have to be the one who makes sure your students keep learning, improving, and living up to their potential. You might be surprised what students can do if you learn to impart valuable criticism.

CHAPTER 14: Age-Related Mistakes to Avoid

It is very important that the rules for your classroom and expectations of the children match up with their ages and capabilities. You neither want to be overly harsh or demanding of young children nor have expectations that are too low for older children.

MISTAKE 116:

Expecting all kindergarteners to know how to behave in a classroom setting...

While many children beginning kindergarten have been in a preschool system or even prekindergarten classroom, you should not expect that all children have been in a classroom setting before. As a kindergarten teacher, you have the privilege of introducing many children to the public or private education system. To some students, you will be their first teacher ever and introduce them to structure like assigned seating, raising their hands to talk, walking in line, and other simple concepts that will soon become second nature to them.

Because some students begin kindergarten already knowing the building blocks of reading or how to write their names, some students will have a better grasp of classroom behavior than others. However, you must assume that they are all lacking in this knowledge, just as you would still teach all students their ABC's even if some students already know them. In short, be patient with those students who defy the structure of the classroom and reiterate the rules whenever necessary. You can also call upon parents to help you remind students of proper classroom behavior and reward students for good behavior.

MISTAKE 117:

Not realizing that puberty can begin as young as 9 or 10...

If you are teaching elementary-aged children, then you probably think you have escaped the age of raging hormones and sexual experimentation. You do not envy your fellow graduates who decided to teach high school, and you are so happy that you will not have to deal with any of the "growing pains" issues your friends will face.

Before you get too smug, there are a few things you should remember. First off, there are several different ways to break students up by age, and they can differ from state to state and from school district to school district. Some smaller areas might group students from K through 8th grade and then have a dedicated high school, while others might group students from K through 6th and then move 7th and 8th graders in with their high school counterparts.

Larger cities and towns usually have some sort of school to transition children between primary (elementary) school and secondary (high) school. This transitional period could cover 7th through 9th grades in a "junior" high school or grades 6th through 8th in a middle school setting. Of course, if you teach at a private school, it is not unusual for you to have all of the grades covered in the same set of buildings/property. It is better to think of the age children begin puberty rather than the grade they begin it.

Of course, you are still correct. By and large, you are off the hook for puberty – particularly if you are teaching the early grades. However, if you are teaching fourth, fifth, or sixth grade, your students will average between 9 and 12 years of age. Some sixth grade teachers might even be blessed with the privilege of teaching a teenager every now and then – children do get held back from time to time.

Now if you begin thinking back to where your body started changing, you will recall that girls can begin their periods at 11 or 12 fairly regularly (and certainly younger). Some girls begin growing breasts around this time, boys' voices might start to change and any of your students could discover hair in never-before-seen places at this age.

While you will hopefully not encounter the "boy crazy" or "girl crazy" stages of puberty while teaching this age group, some students will still be going through some incredibly awkward periods of growth and development. Furthermore, some of your students might not know what to expect about the changes going on in their bodies. Many parents get upset at the idea of sex education being given to elementary students, yet those same parents are highly unlikely to have prepared their 10-year-old daughter for her first period.

Understanding that you could face these challenges and being prepared to deal with them will help you minimize the disruption these "tween" related incidents could cause your classroom. For example, it might be a good idea to have a couple of sweaters from a second-hand shop sitting in your classroom that you can hand a girl to tie around her waist if her first period arrives and catches her completely off guard. This will help her avoid embarrassment and humiliation as you take her to the school nurse.

As you think about your year ahead, if you are instructing children in this age-range, think about all the accidents that could happen and try to prepare for them. If you just cannot wrap your head around this, ask your fellow teachers what they have encountered and how they dealt with it.

MISTAKE 118:

Not approaching parents concerning training bras...

Among the many things you might have to deal with as "tween" girls transition into puberty and their teen years is the fact that some girls will start developing breasts as early as 10 years of age (maybe younger). Even if a girl is a little chubby, the likelihood that the budding breasts under her shirt are just fat is low. If you notice a girl is blossoming without adding a training bra to her wardrobe, you will have to make a decision about talking to her or her parents.

This is another area where you might want to consult other teachers or even ask a guidance counselor or school nurse for some help. However, if the task falls on you, be sure to approach this subject delicately with the parents. Not all parents are prepared to accept that their "little girl" is growing up. You might even be tempted to skip this meeting altogether and let the parents and child figure it out on their own.

The problem arises if the child dresses in such a way that all of the other children can notice she is growing and not dressing accordingly. The first girl to develop in any group of students is always an oddity. She will gather all sorts of attention – and most of it will be negative. Besides whatever discomfort this change causes the girl herself, it will also unquestionably disrupt your classroom. Therefore, if it is not addressed by any other source, then you will eventually need to meet with the parents on the subject.

PART TWO:

RELATIONSHIP MISTAKES TO AVOID

You might be wondering why a book about teaching mistakes would dedicate a large section of its pages to relationships. After all, why do relationships matter in a school setting?

Simply put, how well you relate to your students, their parents, and even your colleagues will matter as much to your career as how well you impart knowledge and skills to your students. Even as you treat your students in an egalitarian manner, you will still form unique relationships with each child because every child is different. One student might take away from your class a love for science, while another student will always remember you as the teacher that helped them finally master their multiplication tables. The different things your students remember you for will be as varied as the reasons you remember them.

Furthermore, you will form relationships with your students' parents on varying levels. Perhaps that relationship will amount to little more than a few teacher conferences a year to go over grades. Or you could get to know the parents of a child very well as you seek to help them deal with a learning disability. But whether you interact with a parent a little or a great deal, relating to them in an effective manner will make your teaching efforts more successful.

These two sets of relationships – with parents and with students – are vital to your success as a teacher. But to optimize your professional achievements, there is one other relationship you should foster as much as possible – the one you hold with your colleagues and administration. Not only can other teachers help you or guide you in handling a difficult situation with a child or parent, they can also help you advance your career. Getting involved in your school at a level you can handle without burning out can help move you from "new kid" to "valued employee" over the course of your first year of teaching. Ignoring these relationships could hurt you when hiring and retention decisions need to be made.

CHAPTER 15:
Classroom Dictator or Mr./Ms. Softie?

Does being liked matter?

For the majority of the individuals reading this book, one thing might be true – you want your students to like you. You probably even want them to love you. Go ahead and admit that and get it out of the way. This book covers 199 mistakes new teachers make and how to avoid them, but wanting to be liked too much is probably at the top of most "Do Not" lists for teachers everywhere.

Wanting to be liked could cause you to be too lax in terms of discipline. It could lead you to use too many "fun" activities in class and not communicate the lesson as well. While you might not want to think of them this way, young children can sense weakness in their supposed leaders. If your students believe they can manipulate you because of your desire to be well liked, this could cause you to lose control of your classroom without even realizing it.

Of course, you do not need to come to the conclusion that the inverse is true – that if wanting to be well liked is a weakness, not caring what your students think must be a strength. No. If you come across as completely unfeeling or uncaring, you will not be able to create a bond with the students, which could make it more difficult for you to engage them in learning. You should not strive to be hated, just like you should not let the children walk all over you just so you will be loved. Read below for how to avoid mistakes at either extreme:

MISTAKE 119:

Wanting to be everyone's favorite teacher...

If you were inspired to become a teacher because of your favorite teacher(s) or because some movie inspired you to teach and make a difference in the lives of your students, being loved by your students probably matters to you a great deal. Even if you have other motives for teaching, you still probably want to be liked by your students – after all, that does making teaching easier and more productive. Besides, who would turn down being named "teacher of the year?"

The most important thing for you to remember as a new teacher is that being loved or liked cannot be your number one objective. You need to earn your student's respect and admiration and being liked – or even loved – will naturally follow. Plan your classroom activities to foster an atmosphere of learning and success rather than "fun", and you will make an impact on the students that will last. You see, it is not the teacher that was entertaining that sticks with you as much as the teacher who finally helped you master multiplication or made sure you could read as well as the rest of your class. Ultimately, you will be remembered for what you taught your students, not how "cool" you were.

MISTAKE 120:

Responding emotionally to a personal attack...

During all the preparation you have done to get ready for your first teaching job, it may have never occurred to you that a student might insult you. If a student gets upset, angry, hurt, or frustrated, then they might say something mean or hurtful to you. Recognizing that this is a possibility, and preparing for it ahead of time could help you keep your cool and maintain a professional demeanor in the face of a painful verbal attack.

If you are teaching young children (five- or six-year-olds), the "mean" thing they say could be as simple as "you are not my mommy" or just an emphatic, loud "no, you can't make me" when you are giving them an instruction. But not all children are raised to be respectful, so you could encounter insults such as "you're fat" or "you're ugly" and other things that might cause you discomfort if you're already feeling vulnerable.

First off, recognize that you are dealing with young children, and they do not have a solid measure of beauty or health or appearance. So resist the urge to wonder if the five pounds you have gained is starting to show or obsess about a blemish you saw in the mirror that morning. The same child that called you ugly one day might say that you are the prettiest girl in the world the next.

My second piece of advice applies to dealing with young children and older children alike; do not take their insults personally. It is far more likely that their insults to you are a reflection of their inability to do their work or frustration over understanding a concept than a testament to what they think about you. While children might be good talkers, they are not necessarily good communicators. They lack the ability to distinguish what is upsetting them and address it. Instead, some will lash out and try to hurt someone else to distract from their feelings of inadequacy. Sadly, some adults do not grow out of this habit.

Even if you do – on some level – take their comments personally, do not show it. Responding emotionally to a student would damage your image of being in control of your classroom and could cause other students to lose respect for you. The best things you can do are to maintain your self-control and address the student's outburst in accordance with your discipline policy for your classroom. If that means sending the child to the principal's office, do so in a calm, controlled manner.

Once you have addressed the outburst from the student, feel free to give your class an assignment that will allow you to regain your composure on the inside if you need to. Halt your lecture and give a reading assignment so you can sit at your desk for a moment and calm down internally. The biggest thing you need to achieve is to not let your students know you were shaken. Do not get angry and yell; do not get hurt and cry.

MISTAKE 121:

Not staying professional when a child is crying...

While both of my children were perfectly fine with me dropping them off their first day of kindergarten and displayed not an ounce of fear or concern, I realize that some children are not so exuberant about this change of life. To encounter crying in a kindergarten class is not unheard of and is probably to be expected.

What you might not be prepared for is that children will cry in all the other grades as well, for a slew of reasons that will not make any sense to you. Consider the following:

Crying over grades. When my daughter was younger, she occasionally cried when she did not make a perfect score on a test. I can only imagine how this mystified her teachers considering she did well – just not perfect. Of course, other students might cry when they fail a test or do badly on an assignment. In any of these cases, you will want to offer them comforting words without minimizing the importance of studying and testing well or doing anything to change the grade they earned.

Crying because they are different. As I have mentioned in other areas of this book, children are keenly aware of what makes them stand out from their classmates. Depending on their personalities, they might like their uniqueness or hate it with a passion. You may find that even without being picked on, a student can feel so uncomfortable about their differences that it can produce tears. If a student admits this is the reason why they are crying, be kind and help them calm down and participate in class again. Do not ever tell them they are crying for a stupid reason – no matter how tempting that might be.

Crying because of rejection. Bullying, teasing, and harassment are certainly things that could make a child cry and must be addressed by you in order to foster a positive atmosphere for learning. However, sometimes your students might not be engaged in these bad behaviors at all, and a child will still feel rejected for one reason or another. If a child feels unpopular or unaccepted or disliked by the girl or boy that they have a crush on, tears can follow. You must deal with these issues quietly and gently so you can minimize the amount of distraction this causes your classroom.

Crying because of home life. Any number of situations could fall into this category, from the kindergartener that misses his mommy to the 10-year-old who just learned her parents are getting a divorce. If a child opens up to you about home, comfort them the best you can and decide if this is a situation that you can handle in the classroom or if they need to see the guidance counselor. Just remember that while you should be considerate of tough times that students face at home, it is still your job to teach them. You can allow these students some extra consideration, but do not pad their grade or forgive poor performance. Not teaching them will not make their home life better and it will do them a greater disservice in the long run. Consult your guidance counselor if you need help figuring out the best way to handle a child going through a tough time at home, and remember to balance the needs of that student with the need to keep your entire class on track academically.

MISTAKE 122:

Letting a classroom get out of hand while having fun...

Every now and then you want to let your students engage in learning activities that are unique and even fun. Just be cautious not to overdo these activities or let them get out of hand. Of course, you want learning to be fun for your students, but you also need to make sure they are still learning. Additionally, you need to tailor your lessons for the age-range you are teaching and the number of students you have in your classroom. An activity that works well with 10 students might get out of hand with 25. Consider the following scenarios:

Multiplication Bean Bag Toss

You create four-by-four or five-by-five boards with the answers to multiplication questions on them and have your students line up behind several boards and see who can toss the bean bag on the correct answer the fastest. I can envision this exercise working well with a handful of students, and I can see it getting totally out of hand in a larger group of kids. Boys waiting in line might toss beanbags at each other. Bored students might call out the answers even if it is not their turn, and what seemed like such a fun way to practice multiplication turns into a disaster for the teacher.

Multiplication Bingo

In this exercise, you create Bingo cards with the answers to multiplication questions on them. You should tell the students the answers will come from their basic multiplication tables and try to use answers that cannot be correct for more than one version (in other words, avoid 16 which can be the answer to 2x8 or 4x4). Or you can use families of multiplication tables such as 8s or 9s to replace the BINGO columns on a normal game card. Either way, you call out the questions (9x5) and allow your students to find the answers on their cards until one of them achieves a "Bingo."

In this scenario, the children are still seated at their desks, but they are allowed to engage their minds in an exercise in an uncommon manner. They are still thinking about and doing multiplication in their heads, it is just being done in the form of a game. Furthermore, if they miss an answer, it does not cost them a grade – it only costs them the chance to win a game. It is a great way for students to learn and make mistakes without it negatively impacting them.

When you examine both of these learning exercises, the beanbag toss probably sounds more "fun," but it is also far more likely to: a) get out of hand and b) fail to teach the lesson you want the children to learn. Having fun is an important element of engaging a child's mind – learning through play they call it – but losing control of your classroom will only lead to play minus the learning altogether.

MISTAKE 123:

Being unwilling to explain yourself...

While you are certainly the king or queen of your classroom and your word is law, so to speak, being unwilling to explain yourself to your students – at least a little – will do you little good in terms of earning and keeping their respect.

You are there to teach, and students are there to learn. If you adopt a complete philosophy of "because I said so," you could be failing to instruct your students. That is not to suggest that you need to explain ad nauseam every classroom policy or decision you make. I am only suggesting that when a student asks "why" it is occasionally OK to explain your reasoning to them.

Furthermore, if a child is asking questions about a subject, there might be a misunderstanding in place between you and your students. If a child has failed to understand a lesson or an action from you, letting that continue could damage the learning process. This is not a question of whether or not you are liked; it is a question of whether or not you are understood.

Do not adopt an attitude of refusing to repeat or explain yourself at all. While you do not want to let your students lead you off course in the middle of a lecture, ensuring that they understand the word or examples you are using is pivotal to communicating your message.

It is understandable that you might not want to allow children to ask questions while you are in the middle of a lecture. Allowing too many questions is a sure way to get derailed and permanently off-topic. If you adopt such a policy, be sure to have a dedicated question and answer time before you cover too much material. Also, evaluate how well your students are engaged at several points during a lecture. If you look out on a sea of confused little faces, it might be time to back up and make sure your students are grasping your meaning.

MISTAKE 124:

Not admitting if you are wrong...

Let us say you had the flu, did not get any sleep, was nearly hit by a very poor driver on the way to school, and broke a nail five minutes before your lecture. So all in all, you have a litany of excuses as to why you suffered the horribly indignity of actually being wrong in front of your class. Still, do not operate as if it did not happen. Correct the error and move on. You are not here to teach your children inaccuracies and misinformation.

MISTAKE 125:

Being too relaxed...

A portion of this book will address mistakes you can make when disciplining a child, but it is important to remember that another discipline mistake can be having none at all. There is a phrase saying that many first-year teachers do not understand until it is too late: "Do not let them see you smile until Christmas."

You are probably wondering why in the world you would want to come across so harsh early on, but the idea is simple – start tough because it is far easier to relax than it is to regain control if you have lost it.

Have a plan for discipline that complies with your school standards and is well communicated to your students. Be prepared to reiterate several times at the beginning of the school year and follow through with it early so students believe that you mean what you say. Remember that making idle threats will not help you build respect. You might think you are being merciful or helping them learn the new system, but in fact you are teaching them that they can get away with breaking your rules to an extent. Instead, make sure you back up your words with deeds.

CHAPTER 16:
Relating to Students that are Different from You

While they say that "opposites attract" when it comes to romantic interests, the truth is that in almost every aspect of your life, you will find it easier to relate to those with whom you have shared interests or similarities than people with whom you cannot find common ground. Shared history, a fandom, even something as small as being born on the same day or finding that you love the same movie can form the basis of a future friendship.

It is not surprising that you will find it easiest to relate to children with whom you share common ground. The students who are different than you are the ones you may find difficult to manage – not because they are poorly behaved or not teachable, but simply because you have more of a gap to bridge. This chapter is dedicated to helping you identify areas where you might need to work a little harder to ensure you are properly reaching your students.

MISTAKE 126:

Continuing the extrovert vs. introvert "war"...

According to Jill D. Burruss and Lisa Kaenzig's article "Introversion: The Often Forgotten Factor Impacting the Gifted" most teachers report being extroverts. This is not very surprising since the school experience – particularly the elementary school experience – is designed to favor extroverts. From an introvert's perspective, the day is full of large common areas and large classes, even bigger groups for lunch and physical fitness, and little to no opportunities to be alone and decompress.

By the time a student reaches high school, they may have enough flexibility to find their down time. They can choose to sit alone at lunch and read for a bit, they can elect to take a study hall in the library, and they can avoid some experiences that would make them the most uncomfortable. But an elementary-aged child does not have that much choice in how to structure their day.

One thing you need to remember is that an introverted child is not just "shy" and in need of being "drawn out of their shell." You do not need to help them make friends with everyone else in the classroom; you only need to help them find their niche. By niche, I mean that even introverted children need to learn certain social skills and they definitely need to be able to participate in class activities.

However, whenever possible, you should incorporate teaching methods that make the introverted student more comfortable in your classroom. At times, allow the introverted child some alone time while other students work in groups. I am not suggesting you purposefully alienate any child, but if you give the children the option of grouping up or working alone, you can watch them decide for themselves what makes them more

comfortable. This is a process you should observe closely and remember for later.

Some suggestions for introverted students include independent study, small group instruction, collaborative learning activities, tiered instruction, role-playing, journaling, quiet time, and book clubs (Burruss 1999). Remaining aware of the fact that children can be introverts and that these children might end up being some of your best students will help you prepare yourself to teach all personalities. If you can be the teacher who helped the introverted child operate at their best rather than try to help them "be like all the other students," you will make a lasting positive impression.

MISTAKE 127:

Not understanding or respecting different religions...

In all likelihood, most of your students will identify with Christianity no matter how often they or their parents attend church. However, even in the smallest of towns, you may have students who are Jewish, Muslim, Buddhist, Hindu, atheist or otherwise. Therefore, when you discuss holidays such as Christmas or Easter, try to remember other holidays that occur during the same time of year and try to be accommodating to students of other religions.

Should you have a student who is an atheist, his or her parents might want you to refrain from participating in holiday activities altogether. Try explaining to these parents that you will not require participation from their child, but that you want to teach traditions pertaining to world religions. This should protect you from perceived favoritism.

Finally, if you identify that one or more members of your class are from a "minority" religion, be sure to understand their traditions and accommodate student absence for their holy days. In fact, you may even need to pay attention to differences between many Christian sects. While all of this might seem like a pain to you, being respectful of varying traditions in a multicultural society will benefit both you and your class.

MISTAKE 128:

Trying to impose your political beliefs on your students...

Young children are sponges, ready to absorb information and opinions and perhaps even adopt them as their own. In fact, political scientists looking to predict election outcomes have polled elementary aged children on who they would elect president and found the correlation to actual results uncanny. The Scholastics News election poll has correctly called 15 of the past 17 presidential elections (Scholastic News Editors, 1996). The simple conclusion is that children accurately reflect the political opinions of their parents, including thoughts about hot-button issues such as abortion, gay marriage, immigration, or support for war.

Even if you are teaching fifth or sixth graders, it is unlikely the child has enough life experience to properly form an opinion about these matters. Therefore, whatever comes out of the child's mouth, they are probably parroting their parents. Should the child say something you strongly disagree with, try not to state your opinion in the classroom. If you want to keep parents on your side, the last thing you need to do is have little Jimmie or Suzie go home and tell them you said they were wrong about hot-button issue x, y, or z.

If the students in your classroom express varying or opposing opinions, you can open the classroom up to discussion of the subject, but be sure to encourage polite debate – not flat out arguing. And be sure to never tell your class who you think is "right" or "wrong."

The one exception to this rule is that you should correct opinions that carry a hint of racism or prejudice in order to make sure all of your students feel comfortable in your classroom. While it is sometimes obvious when a child is a member of a minority, it is not always the case. You should remind your class that it is important to respect other people's religious beliefs, political affiliations, or culture. This could cause some conflict with parents, but you need to stand firm and explain to them that you have students in your classroom from different cultures and it is very important that you create a learning atmosphere free of bullying. Even if they do not like your stance, they will likely support it.

CHAPTER 17:
Recognizing Outside Challenges to Learning

While it would be nice if every classroom were an island to itself so outside influences could not distract from your teaching or your students learning, that is not reality. Some outside influences are internal to the student (such as learning disabilities), while others are external factors (such as a sick sibling or parents divorcing).

It is not your job to solve all of your student's problems, and not matter how much you might want to, you probably will not be able to be their hero if things are going poorly at home. However, you can recognize if these outside influences are affecting a child's work and try to help the student overcome whatever issues or challenges they are facing.

MISTAKE 129:

Assuming a child has a learning disability if they do not...

While you should pay attention to a child's behavior and look for signs that they have a learning disability, you should not quickly assume you know what the child's problem is and allow this conclusion to shape your opinion of the child or how you treat little Jimmy or Suzie.

Instead, you should make notes about the child and their performance. If you have well-structured concerns, bring these issues to the attention of the child's parents and perhaps your campus nurse or counselor (particularly if he or she is a trained psychologist). While you might feel that you see the child often enough to be able to correctly access what medical problems they face, you simple do not know enough about the child's background and medical history to pronounce a child ADHD or bi-polar or autistic. You should leave such diagnosis in the hands of medical professionals who will include you in the process, but only as one voice in drawing their conclusions.

If a parent opposes medication or is resistant to the idea that his or her child has a learning disability, it is important that you do not overstate how strongly you disagree with him or her. Again, let the child's pediatrician walk him or her through this process to determine the best course of action. That way, your relationship with the child's parents is not damaged in any way, and you can more effectively work together to ensure the student can overcome and deal with any learning disability they face.

Additionally, if you are incorrect and there is no learning disability, you might damage your relationship with the parent for no reason. For these reasons, present your observations to the parents without passing judgment.

MISTAKE 130:

Not tailoring work for a child with a physical or learning disability...

Should a child be diagnosed with a learning disability, tailoring their work to accommodate these concerns is vital to your success as a teacher and theirs as a student. Once you have been made aware that a student has a learning disability – whether at the beginning of the school year or later – you need to make any necessary changes that such a disability requires.

Depending on the learning disability the child has been diagnosed with, there could be no change on your part, the child could need to spend time with special teachers, or you might just have to administer some tests verbally instead of in written format. How much you need to adjust to accommodate a student's needs is different in each circumstance, but there is no question you will need plan.

In addition to children with learning disabilities, you might also have a child with a physical disability of some type. For much of my life, I went to school with a girl who was deaf. While we were not always assigned to the same teachers, we did share many classes over the years. I watched her closest friends help her out even when teachers failed to communicate properly with her. She did very well in school and was also named prom queen. I remember her if I ever think about how a student with a physical disability has limits.

Schools have significantly more resources for children with physical handicaps than they did when I was young, but that does not mean you are off the hook for having a child with a disability in your classroom. It is important that you learn how to work with such children to help them achieve their full academic potential.

In order to determine the best course of action for the student, you might need to consult with the child's parents, other teachers, and school resources such as counselors. Follow the advice of your colleagues and make sure you follow any laws or regulations that might be applicable in these instances.

MISTAKE 131:

Dealing with a physical or learning disability inappropriately...

While I am sure that you covered topics like this while earning your degree, I believe it is important to emphasis that a learning disability does not mean a child is stupid. Unless you are a special education teacher, you probably will not be teaching children with severe emotional and intellectual impairments. If a child is in your classroom with a learning disability or physical handicap, it is one that can be overcome in the course of normal academics. Also, even with a learning or physical disability, a child still might be incredibly intelligent.

Hopefully in this day and age, you would not let a child's gender or nationality form preconceived ideas in your head about what the child may or may not achieve. In the same vein, do not let a diagnosis of a learning disability or an obvious physical handicap lead you to conclude a child is not highly intelligent or does not have a strong capacity or appetite for learning.

Keeping an open mind to learn and discover a child's capabilities beyond a learning disability or physical handicap will be an essential part of you being a good teacher to those students. If you conclude early there is something they cannot do or some material they cannot master, you may have falsely limited these children. While you might have to tailor your methods of teaching or testing for the child's individual needs, do not conclude that the child simply cannot learn.

As mentioned above, make sure you work with the parents, experienced colleagues, and school resources (such as the nurse or counselor) to identify a teaching plan that will promote the child's success. Learning disabilities or physical handicaps do not equal a lack of intelligence, and you might find yourself surprised by what your students can achieve if you challenge them to excel.

MISTAKE 132:
Ignoring a sudden drop in grades...

I do not expect that even as your record grades throughout the course of your first year, that you will always know where your students stand in all subjects academically. However, between nine-week grading, progress reports, and just general testing, I do believe you would be capable of noticing if a student suddenly drops in academic performance.

If they only drop off in one subject, and you are tackling new material at that time, then the slip might easily be explained. However, if you notice an all around decline from a student, you might want to consider talking to them about what is going on in their lives, at home, or otherwise that is causing them to have a hard time with their school work.

There are numerous issues the student could be facing to cause a decline in grades, and some of them are actually rather easy to address. At times, children might be facing a difficult home life or even something more serious like molestation. Other times, it could be that the child's eyesight is starting to fail and they need glasses. Whether the problem is complex or simple, making note of a sudden drop in grades and addressing it will do your student a world of good.

I recommend that you begin by talking to the student. Hopefully, little Suzie or Jimmy will quickly confess if questioned that they are having a hard time seeing the board of that the words on the page are starting to look fuzzy. Some students fear anything that will make them look different and the idea that they will need glasses might cause them enough distress that it will take you talking to them and making their parents aware of the situation to get the problem addressed.

Once you rule out concerns like failing eyesight or hearing, you can start to talk to the student about their relationships in the classroom. If the child is being picked on or teased, that can cause a distraction from their work. Something that might signal this problem is if their homework is perfect, but they're testing poorly and doing badly in class. Again, a student should be willing to talk about being bullied if you create a safe atmosphere for them to talk – not with other students present. Feel free to enlist the help of your school counselor as you meet with the student if you think this is the issue.

If you feel like through talking with the student and your general observations of the classroom that the problem the child is facing is not social with their peers, it might be time to ask them about home life. Again, you might want to ask a more experience teacher or your school counselor to sit in on such a meeting. What a child reveals to you could range from their sibling being sick to parents fighting to problems with sexual or physical abuse.

In such cases, you will need to take action, but you will also want to make sure you take the correct action. If you have involved a colleague, they should also be able to help you figure what to do next. Your school counselor and principal should help you determine if law enforcement or other state agencies need to be involved.

The idea of a child confessing to you a serious problem or abuse issue might make you fearful, but it is important that you do not shy away from such challenges as you teach. Your main job might be to educate your students, but you are also there to be their champion and maybe even their hero. Whether you were the first person to recognize they need glasses or the person who gets them the help they need to no longer be abused, you can be the difference in their lives.

So pay attention and do not overlook signs – like falling grades – that something is amiss and needs to be looked at more closely. You will regret it later if you do.

Dealing with children with difficult personal lives

As noted in earlier chapters, a child can face any number of difficulties growing up. There are many stressors and bad things that can happen to children that should never occur, but denial does not make these things go away. A child can face abusive parents, emotional struggles as parents separate and divorce, or just sadness if a parent or sibling is sick.

While you were learning all you thought you needed to know to teach, you might not have been instructed in what to say to a child whose parent is in the military and deployed overseas. You might not have been told what to do if a child's brother is diagnosed with leukemia and all the parent's focus turns to the sick child. No matter how much you know it happens, you might not know what to do for children who are being abused. This section does not have all the answers, but it provides you with stories and advice from teachers who have faced these challenges and lived to tell the tale.

MISTAKE 133:

Favoring one parent over the other during a divorce...

Divorce is hard on children. There is not a way of making it easy on them – even in the most amicable of splits. If one of the parents has been active in supporting the classroom or been the one to always show up at parent/teacher conferences, you might find yourself drawn to support that parent. Or you might have some other bias based on school gossip about why the parents are splitting. You cannot show that to a child or to the parents. Not only is it unprofessional, it does the child no good.

No matter what a child says during a divorce or which parent he or she gets mad at, most likely the child still loves both parents a great deal. He or she does not want to hear bad things about his/her mother or father or hear about how one parent is better than the other. They might want to know whose fault it is, but that is only because they want to know how to fix it. What you need to do is reassure the child that his or her parents love that child and that will not change.

If a child is having a difficult time in your classroom and you know this is going on at home, schedule time for them to talk to your school psychologist. Also, bring the parents in for a conference and talk to them about how they can provide the child the consistency he/she needs to keep doing well in school. While parents sometimes end up using their children to hurt their former partner, most parents only want what is best for the kids even in the middle of the divorce. You cannot fix their marriage, but you can support them as they try to make things easy on their children.

MISTAKE 134:

Not being flexible if the child has stress at home...

You need to be consistent in how you handle children and not show favoritism, but to show zero flexibility when a child is facing a difficult time at home does not advance learning. If a child was sick, you would allow him or her time to make up work. If a child's sibling or parent has a disease or the child is concerned about a parent stationed overseas, this can be far more distracting than getting over the common cold.

In order to reconcile how you work with a student facing a difficult time with the need to be consistent, adopt a general policy of how to handle these situations. Do not allow a child to use a bad situation to not do work or to use your pity to raise his or her grade, but do have an idea of how much time you will allow a child to complete a missed assignment or if you can help them through extra credit. Have a policy that you would offer any child in a difficult situation – after all, odds are good that not all of your kids will be facing a difficult home life simultaneously.

Once you determine how much extra flexibility or time you can afford a child, consult your colleagues and school resources to see what help might be available to the child before or after school. Whether the child needs tutoring or extra time with the school counselor, getting other people involved will help the child get what he or she needs while taking some of the burden off of you to make sure he or she can still succeed academically. You do not have to go through this alone – getting support will be beneficial to both you and the child.

MISTAKE 135:

Basing a child's grades on things they have no control over...

If you are teaching a subject like band where attending a performance is a requirement, it is perfectly reasonable to factor that into your student's grades. However, be sure not to base too much of your student's grades on events that occur outside of the classroom.

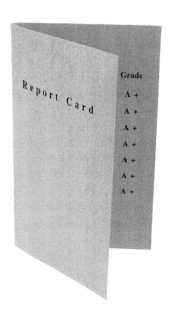

Your students are young children who cannot control their parents' schedules or ability to take them to mandatory events. Furthermore, they also cannot control events such as traffic, car breakdowns, illness, and any number of other reasons why they might end up missing a performance.

As such, while it is important to teach children the value of following through on commitments, be sure to allow your students to be excused for missing mandatory events if their parents offer you a legitimate reason for their absence.

MISTAKE 136:

Promising silence if a child confides in you...

The things a child could tell you in secret range from the heartbreaking (the little sister has cancer) to the infuriating (someone is touching them where they should not). It might be hard to break a promise to a child, to violate their trust when they confide in you, but sometimes that is exactly what you must do. If you are unsure how to do it, seek help from a coworker or school therapist.

There are protocols you can take to intervene in the proper way and those steps should be followed. If the end result of you revealing the information a child shares with you is going to be a prosecution, then you need to work with the police to make sure they are able to build a strong case against the wrongdoer.

No matter how anonymous you might want to remain, even if you have to break your word to a child, someday they will understand.

When the situation is just one that is sad rather than something that needs official interference, you might be free to keep the child's secret. However, if you start to feel uncomfortable or get the impression that the parents should be made aware of their child's feelings, talk to the school counselor on if/how you might approach them or try to talk the child into approaching their parents themselves.

MISTAKE 137:

Not seeking help from the school counselor...

If you have a trained child psychologist on staff, it seems like a waste not to consult them on any issue you are not sure how to deal with in regards to your students. Your school's guidance counselors are not just an asset to you because of their experience, but also because of their training. There is little reason for you to try to figure out every situation by yourself.

While not every guidance counselor will have experienced every challenge a child could endure, they likely have more first-hand experience and training in this area than you do at this point in your career. Seek their help not just to protect yourself and your career, but also because helping children through difficult periods of time is why they work for the school.

CHAPTER 18:
Relating to Parents/ Guardians

If you thought being a teacher only meant working with children, then you have missed half the equation. Parents are your partners in education and should provide you with all the support you need to maximize your teaching efforts for their children. While that might not always be the case, you should still give parents every opportunity to engage with you and be an active component in their child's academics.

Furthermore, the relationship you form with the parents of your students can have a great impact on both the student's performance and the impression your principal forms on your work. If you develop a negative relationship with some of the parents, that can cast a dark shadow on your classroom and lead to several complaints finding their way to your boss. While you do not want to walk on eggshells in fear of what parents might say about you, you do need to keep in mind the downside of bad people skills in your profession. In order to maximize the likelihood that parents will end up singing your praises to the principal at the end of the year, avoid the mistakes described below:

Communicating with parents regarding grades and student progress

You might think that if you are having no behavioral issues in your classroom than there is no reason to contact parents. You would be wrong. While parents might consider "no news – good news" when it comes to bad behavior, many appreciate proactive communications when it comes to grades. Parents do not want to be blindsided at the end of the year with your impression that a child should be held back. Nor do they want to only hear about a child not doing their homework after they see a "D" on a report card.

Whether or not a parent is highly communicative with you, most assume that you will make them aware of issues they need to act on. If you notice that a child is late to school frequently, missing classes too often without notes from the parent, or other behavior that could lead to the child failing, go ahead and call the parents.

MISTAKE 138:

Not communicating with parents in writing...

If you are having trouble with a student, be sure to communicate with the parent – in writing – what your issues are and the potential punishment the child faces. If you can send e-mails, save your side of the communication and request an e-mail receipt. If you can only leave  them messages or send notes, keep dated copies of your communications to show your efforts to reach out to the parents.

While it is not pleasant to think of a parent filing a complaint against you, some adults are more likely to blame the teacher than hold their children accountable for behavioral issues. The more you can do to prove you tried to reach out to the parents, the less they will be able to argue against you at a later date.

MISTAKE 139:

Not sending work/tests home regularly...

As I mentioned before, many parents are actually excited to see the results of their children's work. Additionally, you really do not need a backlog of student work taking up space on your desk. Make every effort to regularly grade, record, and send home tests and assignments.

MISTAKE 140:

Waiting too long to update parents on grades...

If you send work home regularly, you might think you are keeping parents well enough appraised on their children's grades. However, keep in mind that parents do not know how you weight grades or what classroom assignments could be pulling a grade up or down. Do not wait until a nine-week grading period is nearly complete to warn a student – or their parents – that they are in danger of making a poor grade. Send home progress reports and if you notice a child make several poor test grades, tally up where they stand at that point and keep parents notified. It is important that you give students every opportunity to work to bring their grades up.

MISTAKE 141:

Not reporting behavioral issues...

Even if you are just having minor behavioral issues with a student in the classroom, you should still send a note home to their parents. It is very frustrating from a parent's point-of-view to deal with an escalated situation when you heard nothing about the little steps that lead to the "crisis" along the way. Be sure to communicate with parents when you are having issues, you might find those problems are easily corrected just by letting the parent know what is going on at school.

MISTAKE 142:

Not scheduling parent-teacher conferences...

It is very important to schedule parent-teacher conferences on a semi-regular schedule. You may want to do it when it is time to send home progress reports or report cards. Or you might want to schedule conferences just with the parents who have concerns. No matter what your strategy is, be sure to leave yourself open whenever a parent might want to meet with you.

MISTAKE 143:

Waiting too long to tell parents you think there is a learning problem...

Part of building a solid relationship with parents means establishing an open line of communications early and keeping it flowing throughout the school year. When a child is excelling and demonstrating excellent behavior, it is easy to talk to parents. However, you might feel intimidated when the student starts to slip in behavior or grades. You might have even heard horror stories of parents blaming the teacher for the child's bad performance and feel that any communication might spell confrontation.

The first thing you need to do is relax. Talking to and working with parents can be more beneficial than you can imagine. In the majority of cases, no one knows a child's strengths or weaknesses better than his or her parents. They might be able to provide you with insight that can help you improve the child's performance, and you can provide them with guidance on what they can do at home to help their child succeed.

The mistake of not communicating with parents early on only gets worse if the child's performance continues to slide. I have a good friend who still speaks ill of one of his daughter's kindergarten teacher years later because that teacher never mentioned a problem with the child's learning or academic progress until the end of the year when she called him in to discuss holding the child back. He insists that progress reports and report cards never indicated his daughter was struggling, and he had no idea that the teacher felt his daughter was lagging behind until it was nearly too late to do anything about it.

Of course, I cannot speak about the teacher's point-of-view in this instance, but assuming this parent is telling the tale close to the truth, there was a serious break-down of communications between teacher and parent in this case. Additionally, that parent might have a real complaint to bring to that teacher's supervisor. If you are in your first year of teaching, you definitely do not want to get caught in this situation.

Remember that your first priority should be helping the child achieve academic success. Even if the parent proves unresponsive, your attempts at communication will prove that you have done all you can to advance the success of all of your students. Even if you do this for no other reason than to protect yourself, I believe you will find it immensely beneficial in the long run.

MISTAKE 144:

Blaming parents for not supporting a student at home...

The last thing you want to do with a parent is be confrontational, even if you are upset with them for the lack of support they show a child at home. When you sit down with a parent that you feel is not providing your student the right amount of support, do not lecture them on what they are failing to do for the child.

First, that is likely to create an adversarial exchange where they blame you for their student failing instead of listening to what you have to say. Second, it really will not help solve the problem. You need explain in what areas the child needs to improve, how they can help the child improve, and what the student needs to do better.

Communicating with the parents openly may or may not change the support the child receives at home, but blaming the parent for the child's failures will not help the situation either. In order to keep positive relations going between you and the parents, keep things cordial. Try not to be overly judgmental on their parenting, and then perhaps they will not be unfairly judgmental on your teaching.

MISTAKE 145:

Blaming the parents if a child is badly behaved at school...

Many people feel that if a child is bad, the parents are doing something wrong. While it might be the case that your most ill-behaved or spoiled child is the product of over-indulgent parenting, it will do you little good to approach parents for help with a child's behavior while playing the "blame" game.

On occasion, we have to put the responsibility of a child's behavior squarely on the child's shoulders. The older the child, the more likely the possibility that bad behavior is coming from the student's own desires, choices, or motivations. A student can be motivated by the desire to "be cool" or to impress a girl/boy. They can also be acting "tough" because they are afraid of getting picked on.

If a child is a disruption in your class, the best approach is to try to work with the parents to correct the situation. Should you come to believe that the parent is part of the problem, you will have to work around that situation. Still, avoid treating the parent with contempt even if they do not act as your immediate ally. Things can change and cultivating a positive relationship with the parents might prove beneficial to you – or a fellow teacher – down the road.

MISTAKE 146:

Not clearly communicating how a student can improve...

In addition to not blaming a parent for a student's poor grades, you must also accept that the responsibility of communicating what the student needs to work on and how they can improve his or her grades is really on you.

There are many intelligent, dedicated parents out there who will look over a child's grades and tests and work to identify what their child is doing poorly in. If they can properly identify what their child does not understand, then these parents might even be willing and able to work with their child to correct their poor performance. **These parents are not the norm.**

Most parents will expect that you are strictly their child's teacher, and it is your job to teach them. The average "engaged" parent will probably make sure their child gets their homework completed and may even go over their homework with him or her to make sure they got everything correct. That same parent might even review some study material with their children before a test, but parents have their limits. These limits often come out during science projects, so tread lightly there.

If parents start to feel like they are doing more work with their child than you, then they might become bitter and resentful. "I should just home school my child for all the work I do them with after school" or "Exactly who is teaching my child, me or their teacher" are shared sentiments among many parents I know. You really do not want to contribute more to the idea that teachers are not doing their jobs during your first year of teaching.

When you communicate with the parents of your students in regards to grades (be it on progress reports or at parent/teacher meetings), be sure to explain to the parents what little Jimmy or Suzie can do to improve. Furthermore, if one of your students is performing particularly poorly in a subject or two, be sure to communicate information to the parents regarding after-school help or tutoring.

If you approach parents in this manner and provide them with tools to help their children improve, then you will create a feeling of teamwork and collaboration between you and the parents. That sense of cooperation is the best thing you can do to help your students thrive, and it will prevent a host of complaints about you later if you have to counsel a parent to hold back a child.

MISTAKE 147:

Not telling the parents if you think the child might have a learning disability...

You are new to your job, and this might even be the first time you have worked with a large group of students on your own. You certainly do not have a psychology degree, and you are not a medical doctor. So if you observe behavior in a child that might be considered indicative of a learning disability, do you speak up about it? Would the parents listen to your opinion? If other teachers have not noticed this and talked to the parents by now, are you even sure you are right about this?

These questions and doubts are all perfectly reasonable in your first – or even first several – years of teaching. It is one thing when a teacher with 20 years of experience who has worked with hundreds of students tells a parent "I think you should have little Tommy tested for dyslexia." It is quite another when a 20-something-year-old tells a parent that his or her child might have ADHD. Right?

Perhaps the older, more experienced teacher does have a better foundation to form their opinion. And perhaps the parents will not listen to you. You could even be wrong. But sharing your concerns and thoughts about a child's behavior or challenges in your classroom with the parents is never a bad idea. If anything, talking to the parents could be the beginning of a discussion they need to have with their doctors and other professionals, or it could be the last note of confirmation they need to tell them what they have already suspected.

While it would serve you well to consult other teachers in the school and/or the school guidance counselor and nurse, it is in the end up to you to sit down with the parents and tell them your concerns. You do not need to present your opinion as fact to these parents – after all, you lack the expertise to be sure of anything. But opening up the lines of communications with the parents is not a mistake, and you might learn something from the parents that explains the behavior you have noted.

MISTAKE 148:

Letting your personal opinion of a parent show...

It takes all kinds of people to make the world go 'round. You will have parents you think poorly of for many reasons. You will see mothers who dress like prostitutes, and you will have fathers you think look completely unkempt. You will also see fathers or mothers with new wives or husbands that seem far too old or too young to have a kid.

There will be parents who do not answer your calls or emails. There will be parents who are argumentative or rude to you. On the other hand, there will be parents who are influential in your town or obviously wealthy. There will be parents who drive fancy cars or wear expensive jewelry. There might even be parents who could do you personal favors.

For good or bad, do not allow your opinions of parents to show to your students. Treat all of the parents with the same professional regard and respect. Not only do you need to make sure the parents do not pick up on any favor or disdain you have for them, but more importantly, you need to make sure the students do not figure out who you like or dislike.

Young children will probably think their parents are amazing. But the older that children get, the more they will become aware of the social norms of their community. They will be able to look around and see if one parent dresses different (better or worse) than the rest. Children will be able to figure out rather easily whose parents are impressive and whose are not. What you want to do is maintain an aura of being neither impressed nor put-off to your students.

The reason that this is important is that children cannot help if they are born into a poor family or a well-off one. They have no control over how their parent dresses or speaks. They do not deserve to be looked down upon or respected solely because of their parents. If you send cues to your students that you have an overly strong positive or negative opinion of their parents, you might inadvertently make the child believe that opinion carries over to them.

You want to make sure that your children believe the classroom is a place of equality. A place where if they work hard, they can receive the grade they deserve. You do not even want to create the illusion that some children are favored or held back because of their parents. Treating all parents the same will help your students realize that you are judging them for them – not their parents.

How to deal with divorced parents

Dealing with parents is difficult enough, dealing with parents who do not like each other or work together is even harder. Unfortunately, with the marriage success rate in the U.S. being about 50/50, the chances that you will have students with divorced parents or even parents going through a divorce during the school is year is likely. You must figure out how to navigate this minefield with grace and a strong focus on what is best for your student.

While the parents will be dealing with loads of negative feelings, they will not always be keeping their focus on what is in the best interest of their children. Even the most well-meaning parents will have lapses and failures in this regard (and of course, not all parents have the best of intentions). In order to avoid having parents dislike and be uncooperative with you, read on for some basic strategies on dealing with divorced parents.

MISTAKE 149:

Communicating with one parent, but not the other...

In most divorce situations, friends and family will be forced to "choose sides." You are the one exception to that rule. Not only is there no need for you to favor one parent over the other, but it is also ill-advised for you to do so.

You will encounter both the parents who are already divorced and those who are going through one. No matter how custody is split between the parents, unless one parent has a court order disallowing the other information regarding their child, it is best that you keep the lines of communications open with both the mother and father.

That does not mean you need to send two sets of paperwork home so the child can take it to both sets of parents. But if you send email notifications to your parents, be sure to include both parents on those lists. Make sure you schedule parent teacher conferences with both the mother and the father if you need to communicate with them regarding grades or behavioral issues. Try to make sure they both know about school events, such as plays and holiday events.

Parents have a lot of work to do in a divorced setting to make sure the child does not need to choose between his/her parents. How parents decide to split up school functions is really up to them. You just need to do your job and make sure information is communicated to both parties and let them figure out the rest.

MISTAKE 150:

Appearing to favor one parent over the other...

If you know a parent because they are highly involved with their child's schooling (say they have brought in cupcakes on a birthday and chaperoned a field trip), you might be tempted to favor them if a divorce occurs. Or you might see bad behavior during the divorce and come to favor the other parent as a result. Worse yet, you might have really been friends with the couple before you taught their child, and you have a natural loyalty to one of the two parents.

None of this matters when it comes to professionalism and how you should conduct yourself as their child's teacher. Communicating with both parents is still important, being considerate of both parents is still important, and engaging both parents in a positive way when you see them is still important. Do not allow the drama of divorce to enter into your classroom.

Furthermore, while little Timmy or Sarah might be very upset with one of their parents, they still love them very much. Your student does not want to think that one parent is the "bad guy" and if you appear to take sides in this conflict, you could damage your relationship with your student without even realizing it. And even if you do not negatively impact your relationship with the student, you will almost certainly destroy it with the parent whom you badmouthed. To do your job well, you need a positive working relationship with both parents – especially during a divorce. Always keep that in mind.

MISTAKE 151:

Being unwilling to communicate with a step-parent...

While I have advised you to be Switzerland when it comes to divorced parents, and I can certainly understand you not wanting to get involved with parent and step-parent bickering, you still need to proceed with caution when it comes to keeping a step-parent out of the loop.

When you talk to a student, you might find that it is their step-parent who does his or her homework with the child or the step-parent who helps him or her study for tests. If this is the case, not speaking to a step-parent because an offended mother or father does not like you doing so will hurt your student more than help him/her. Think of it this way: if the schooling parent hired a tutor for little Jimmy or Suzie, would you refuse to talk to that tutor just because the other parent did not like it? If the answer is "of course not," then think of the step-parent in the same light.

If you are concerned about issues of confidentiality or privacy, consult with your school's principal. Most likely, all you need to know is what the custody arrangement is and if one legal guardian has consented for you to consult the step-parent. Again, if other legal issues are present, your principal can help you work it out.

In the worst-case scenario, you might be unable to talk to the step-parent because the school does not want to risk getting sued or dragged into the court battle. But you should not be unwilling to work with step-parents when it benefits your student and you are able to do so.

Teaching Family

If you find yourself teaching in the town you grew up in (which is quite common), the chances are good at some point that you will teach a family member. The family member could be as close as your own child or niece/nephew or more distant like your cousin's children. When this occurs, your first instinct should be to request the school reassign the student. If that cannot be accommodated, you should take precautions not to be perceived as unfair or biased.

MISTAKE 152:

Not making administration aware of the relationship...

Of course, the first mistake you can make is not making administration aware of the relationship between you and the child. They can hardly try to rearrange the classrooms if they do not know there is a potential area of conflict.

MISTAKE 153:

Letting the child call you by a name the other students cannot use...

If you do end up having to teach a family member, let them know that while they might call you "Aunt Trish" at home, in the classroom, they need to address you as "Mrs. Robinson." You are not doing this as an attempt to hide your relationship with the child from your other students, but just trying to leave the impression that all children in your classroom are on even footing.

MISTAKE 154:

Working too hard not to show favoritism...

While you need to make every effort not to show favoritism to a family member, do not go too far in the other direction and become unnecessarily harsh toward or ignore the child to whom you are related. Parents who coach their own children tend to vacillate back and forth between wanting to make their kid the "star" unfairly and being harder on their child than anyone else on the team. Your goal is to treat your family member the same as your other students, not better or worse.

CHAPTER 19:
Relating to Other Teachers

One of the most valuable assets available to a new teacher is other, more experienced teachers. Chances are good that no matter what shocking or challenging situation arises during your first year of teaching, one of your colleagues has experienced the same issue and will have some advice to help you handle it. Therefore, it stands to reason that forming and maintaining good relations with your fellow teachers is an important part of your professional development. This chapter will offer guidance on mistakes to avoid in your efforts to create solid working relationships at your school.

MISTAKE 155:

Not asking for guidance if you need it...

If you are reading this book, then you are clearly interested in avoiding mistakes. Your first year of teaching – well, any year of teaching, really – can be full of challenges and at times overwhelming. Many first-year teachers get burnt out and are just plain exhausted long before they get to summer vacation. If you get tired or frustrated, your students will suffer. Do not be afraid to ask for advice and use it (and sick days – you get to use those too when you need them).

One of the biggest mistakes inexperienced teachers – well, professionals of any kind, really – make is wanting to cover up their inexperience so much that they do not ask for help from their colleagues or supervisors. You coworkers and supervisors can help you and in many cases, they have quick, easy advice to give you that can make your life easier. Ask questions, seek guidance, and leverage your associates' ideas so you can be better at what you do.

MISTAKE 156:

Getting involved in school politics...

Schools have their own versions of "office politics" and getting involved in them can prove detrimental to any teacher, but especially so to the "new guys on the block." Just as your students might have squabbles, grudges, and backstabbing, so might your coworkers. The best action you can do is to steer clear and stay quiet.

If there are instances where you have a "vote" in a matter, listen carefully to what others have to say about the individuals up for a position and participate in the election, but do so without drawing attention to yourself.

MISTAKE 157:

Getting caught up in gossip...

Like any work environment, gossip will circulate at school. People will discuss each other's personal lives, professional behavior, and at times cross lines that should not be crossed. While technically talking about anyone behind  his or her back can constitute gossip, there is definitely positive and negative talk. Discussing how you love someone's idea for a fundraiser is vastly different than speculating why someone's husband never comes to school events.

While it might seem like listening to campus gossip is an easy way to start to fit in and bond with your co-workers, it could prove detrimental to your working relationships or even your career. Even if gossip seems harmless, it can lead to you getting caught up in the campus politics mentioned in the previous entry and make you someone that another teacher now has a grudge against.

Also as you will recognize with your own students, your reputation will be shaped by the company you keep – so just listening to someone else gossip can hurt you. Find a way to politely excuse yourself from conversations when this sort of activity comes up. Do not be concerned about what people will say behind your back when you leave the room. Just conduct yourself as you should, and soon you will earn the respect of your colleagues.

As an addendum to this mistake, do not gossip with other teachers about students or parents. OK, yes, students talk about you – parents do as well. And yes, by the time I graduated high school, I realized that teachers talk about students and parents, too. It takes place in just about every teaching lounge across the country. However, it is still best to avoid and can cause problems – and if you are new, it is far more likely to hurt your career than help it.

MISTAKE 158:

Passing along a false allegation...

One of the worst side effects that can come from gossiping is passing along a false allegation. Whether the allegation comes from a student, parent, or another teacher if it is something that should be brought to a principal or supervisor – do it and then wait and see what happens.

Reputations can be damaged in an instant and take an eternity to repair. Even being vindicated from a false allegation cannot always repair a damaged reputation. While there are some things that cannot be ignored, it is best that you do not help convict someone of something before all the facts are known. If a teacher is accused of misconduct, abuse, sexual harassment, and other inappropriate behavior, your best course of action is to make the necessary report and let management take action. Just understand that accusations are not always true and spreading gossip will not benefit you if turns out to be a false report.

If, after watching management's course of action, you decide the situation was handled badly, you might need to make some decisions on going over your supervisor's head or going to the school board. But that is a worst-case scenario that you will hopefully never face – especially not in your first year of teaching. And even in that case, gossip will not help you. You might need to seek advice, but do so one-on-one with someone you respect and trust.

CHAPTER 20:
Teaching in a Politically Correct World

On the flip side of the same coin of favoritism is showing disdain for any one student or group of students. The first thing you should probably ask yourself is if you do have any preconceived ideas about people based on race, gender, religion, etc. I am not asking you to call yourself any of those "ist" you want to avoid being labeled by parents or administrators. I'm suggesting you ask yourself if you are prepared to teach children of all races, religions, and even sexual orientations.

No, I am not talking about the children's parents – I am talking about the children themselves. Children today – even young ones – are being encouraged to explore their gender identity, different religious options, and even how they define themselves in terms of race (mixed-race children might identify themselves one way or another or as both). Besides wanting to avoid making mistakes that could land you in sensitivity training or being officially reprimanded, you need to be prepared to treat all of your students equally and not interfere with how the parents are raising their children – no matter what your personal opinion may be.

MISTAKE 159:

Letting your religion show...

The percentage of atheists in the U.S. is relatively small, so it is safe to conclude that the majority of us are people of faith. But we are not people of the same faith. Even among those who practice the same faith, there are variations on the theme. While I understand that some religions teach their practitioners to live their life as a witness, evangelizing in the classroom is a mistake and could get you fired.

Furthermore, you should go ahead and dismiss any negative ideas you have of other faiths before you come face-to-face with a child being raised in that faith and say something to offend. When you lecture on religious groups in history, be sure to use facts, not opinion. It is a fact to say that a Pope was once so powerful that he was able to order a Crusade into the Holy Lands. It is conjecture to suggest that Catholics were once justified in killing Jews and Muslims. Even if the latter is reasonably safe to assume based on the truth of the former, it is best for you to present history in terms of facts and let your students draw their own conclusions.

If you happen to be one of the few atheists in the U.S., it is equally damaging for you to let any disdain you feel for the religion your students practice show. Debating on matters of faith and whether or not there is a God is best saved for college campuses and coffee houses, not a fourth-grade classroom. No matter what you think of a student's spiritual beliefs, keep it to yourself.

One final note in this area, you should show respect for other faith's holidays and customs. Children of all religions will be excused from school to observe their holy days. Do not act as if you cannot be bothered to accommodate their schedules or demand the completion of an assignment directly after a religiously excused absence. No matter how annoyed you might feel that every faith's high holy days cannot be concentrated into spring, winter, and summer breaks, do not allow this annoyance to cause you to commit mistakes in how you treat your students.

MISTAKE 160:

Only celebrating "common" holidays...

As a tangent to the issue of religion, do not tell your class you are only going to celebrate "real" holidays or "American" holidays or anything else like that. While you might just be looking to celebrate the secular Christmas, it would not do you any harm to spend part of a day discussing how so many world religions have special holidays at the same time of year. Then you can also discuss the different legends that arose around Christmas throughout the world. Using an approach like this should allow you to experience the holidays with your students without offending any minority group in the process.

MISTAKE 161:

Letting stereotypes show up in your classroom...

Even when you are teaching young children, you need to make sure you – and your students – check their stereotypes at the door. Even if the stereotype seems positive – like all Asians are good at math and science – it has no place in your classroom. You are there to teach children who will have varying degrees of talent in science, history, math, language, music, athletics, reading, art, and more. You need to create an atmosphere where each student can discover where their talent lies and exactly what their strengths and weaknesses will be.

If you approach teaching or allow your students to approach learning from a point of preconceived notions not based on performance, you will limit your children from the start. If you find yourself thinking a student will be good or bad at something based on nothing else but their gender or ethnicity, dismiss that notion completely and discover if the child is talented in that area or not.

MISTAKE 162:

Treating girls and boys differently...

At the time this book was written, NFL athletes were making headlines for domestic abuse. It was an incredibly embarrassing time for the NFL as they worked out exactly how they should deal with the issue, and what punishment, if any, they were responsible for giving their players. One of the most common responses to the discussion about domestic violence is that a man never has a right to hit a woman, regardless of the situation..

Translate this idea to elementary-aged children and you get the message that it is OK if little Suzie socks little Timmy in the mouth, but little Timmy is not allowed to do anything to defend himself. If you allow this mentality to seep into your classroom, you will establish the precedent for children to think of girls and boys and being different and there being one set of rules for girls and another set of rules for boys.

It is as simple as that. The battle of the sexes begins in grade school as does the simple question – are we equal or not? No matter what your personal opinion on this matter is, legally you are required to create a classroom atmosphere where the genders are considered equal. Since that is your responsibility, I recommend that you dispense with the old ideas that girls can hit boys, but boys cannot hit girls and other such nonsense. Discipline children equally for equal offenses and you will send the message clearly to your students that you do not believe girls are better than boys or vice versa.

This is important not just for maintaining your classroom and avoiding sensitivity training, it is vital to the learning process as well. While the pendulum has certainly been swinging, certain college majors and industries are still predominately thought of as "male" or "female." If you have a girl who is good in science or a boy who is good at art, you do not want old fashioned ideas of what girls and boys should be doing to seep into your classroom and poison a child against pursuing an area of natural talent.

The more ways you can communicate equality between the genders, the less likely it will be that your students will come to think of an area of learning to be for "boys" or "girls." This will ultimately allow your students the best possible learning environment, and it should be your goal for every class you teach.

MISTAKE 163:

Not protecting students who may be gay...

It certainly seems unlikely you will have to deal much with the issue of children's sexuality in grade school, but some people claim to have known there was something "different" about them even when they were very young. More importantly though, with sexuality and gay marriage becoming a more common topic today, children are more aware of how they can accuse each other of being "gay" without fully understanding what that means.

Make sure that you recognize if a child is being bullied because she is too much of a "tomboy" or because he is too "sissy." While girls and boys are different and any endeavor to create a gender neutral world is futile, you should still make sure that children are not being made fun of because of antiquated ideas of what it means to be a boy or girl. Just because a boy likes pink and crafts does not mean he is going to grow up to like other boys. Not allowing your students to perpetrate foolish ideas like that or attach negative feelings to the idea of being gay will do a lot to protect the self-esteem of any child in your room that may later come out.

MISTAKE 164:

Allowing students to make fun of a child's accent or culture...

Some children have a tendency to find anything that is different amusing or tease-worthy. A child who has a heavy accent or dresses differently because of their family's culture could be subject to ridicule or scorn. You should do what you can to put a halt to that type of behavior in your classroom and teach respect to all of your students.

MISTAKE 165:

Not helping children who live in poverty keep up with the class...

Some families can barely afford clothes and shoes to send their children to school. Be aware of your student's financial backgrounds before you send home assignments that require even small purchases. And if a student tells you that he or she could not complete an assignment because they did not have the supplies, be sympathetic and provide them with an alternate opportunity. I know you will not always be able to supply your class on your budget, but be aware that parents have budgets too – and some of them are incredibly tight.

PART THREE

PROFESSIONAL MISTAKES TO AVOID

As a new teacher, you probably have – at most – a one-year contract. No matter how secure a teacher's position with tenure may be, you could do your job perfectly and still not be renewed the following year. Follow the advice in this section to give yourself the best shot at a more permanent contract.

CHAPTER 21:
Choosing Your School Environment

This book would not be complete without at least some words of caution when it comes to selecting the school you where you will work. Your first thought might be to accept whatever job comes your way and you may need to do so in order to get your career started. However, if you do have a choice, keep in mind some of the differences that come with public/private schools.

MISTAKE 166:

Not understanding how different types of public schools work...

Public schools have come under increased criticism in recent years, but they are still the most prevalent form of education offered in the US. If you work in a public school environment, government mandates can impact your curriculum choices and you may find yourself having to meet a lot of requirements that you do not entirely understand. If you teach in a state with mandatory testing, you may find yourself feeling burdened by having to ensure your students achieve a certain level of test scores.

The charter school is a branch off the traditional public school in that it is still funded by the government, but it operates without many of the regulations affecting normal public schools. These alternative institutions were first launched in the 1990s and they can provide a different type of school structure to their students. Generally speaking, charter schools seem to have been proven successful in providing a better education and student experience.

As a teacher at a charter school, you might have fewer students per class, more freedom to design your curriculum, and your job will be tied to the school's success. If the school fails to meet the requirements of their charter, it could close. When you are applying to different schools and eventually accept your first job, be sure you understand the rules and regulations you will be operating under for your first year of teaching.

MISTAKE 167:

Not understanding the requirements of various private schools...

If your first teaching job is at a private school, you too must understand the unique standards you will be expected to meet. Private schools can vary dramatically in their setup and core beliefs. These can include preparatory schools where parents send their children with the expectation that the school will prepare their children for college, military academies, and religious schools.

Being hired at any one of these schools will come with certain expectations. If you happen to agree with the school's ideology, you will probably fit in just fine. But if you have issues where you disagree with what the school teaches, you will need to decide ahead of time how to deal with that or you could risk your job.

CHAPTER 22:
Behavioral Mistakes

Throughout this book, we have covered several things you should not do. But this chapter is dedicated to compiling in one place several mistakes you could make in regards to how you behave on the job. If you can avoid these mistakes, you should be able to prevent any serious issues of discipline or reprimand.

MISTAKE 168:

Using language not fit for children to hear...

I dedicated a section to how you should avoid cursing in front of your students, but you should probably avoid inappropriate language at work altogether. While I am sure many teachers will use more adult language in their break room, it is probably best that you try not to flip back and forth between knowing when you can and cannot say certain things.

Note that there are words that might not be considered "curse" words, but they should still be excluded from your vocabulary completely. From racial slurs to gender-specific insults, you probably already know the words and phrases you should avoid. Remember that just like there is appropriate attire for work and "going out" clothes you can wear with your friends, your language needs to follow the same rules. Just because you use a word with your friends and do not think anything of it, does not mean you can speak like that at work. When in doubt, err on the side of caution.

MISTAKE 169:

Showing prejudice or bias...

Just like any professional environment, you have to comply with certain standards and expectations. One of the biggest ways you could get yourself in trouble is to demonstrate racism, sexism, or any other bias that could be perceived by your students or coworkers.

You should assume there is no "safe" prejudice you can demonstrate in the workplace. We live in a far more diverse world than before, and even the smallest towns may have students who are Muslim, Indian, or the children of two mommies. No matter what your opinion is on race, religion, gay marriage, or nationality, you should probably make it a point to not make disparaging remarks to your students or coworkers about any minority group.

Furthermore, in your efforts to minimize bullying in your classroom and school, it would be best for you to lead by example and not make jokes at anyone's expense. When a child sees you crack a joke at someone's expense, they may think it is safe for them to do so. Being careful in this regard will set the right tone for your classroom and protect you professionally.

MISTAKE 170:

Getting political...

If you are a new hire during an election year, that is probably not the right time for you to be really vocal about your political opinions or who you are supporting in local school board elections. I am not saying you need to bite your tongue forever when it comes to politics. But I am suggesting that when you are new to the work environment, you have no way of knowing who is friends with whom. The last thing you want to do is express negative opinions of someone who wins an election to someone who knows that candidate.

When it comes to politics—local and national—my advice during your first year of teaching is to listen to the opinions of those around you without overtly stating your own. Particularly when it comes to school board or superintendent elections, take the time to get to know why your fellow teachers support one candidate over another. Listening to your colleagues may help you form or reform your own opinion while ensuring you do not leave a negative impression on those who know more about the school district and personnel than you do.

MISTAKE 171:

Dressing inappropriately...

Your school likely has a dress code for you to adhere to and there will be scheduled days for casual wear. However, you should likely do more than meet the dress code early in your career. Career coaches have loads of advice to share with candidates on how to dress for interviews. And I have heard of people not getting a job simply because they did not meet a certain standard for interview attire.

It is almost disturbing to think that qualifications can be damned if a dress code is not properly met. However, in today's market where there are more qualified candidates than job slots, every bit of distinction can separate one person from another. And during your first year, you are in many ways still a job candidate.

Therefore, it will probably serve you well to dress a little nicer than required throughout the school year. There will certainly be times when wearing a school t-shirt and jeans is more than appropriate, but otherwise, dress it up rather than down.

MISTAKE 172:

Dating someone on the staff...

Of all the places a single person can meet someone to date, work is the number one location for most. However, dating someone in the workplace is usually frowned upon, even in the corporate environment. At a school, you might have fewer opportunities, but it is an equally bad idea.

If you meet someone at the school, date, and eventually marry, everything could come up roses. However, if you end the relationship at some point, it could create a very awkward work environment for both of you. As a new teacher, you do not need to add stress to an already stressful job. It is for the best that you keep your work and personal life separate and date outside of the school.

MISTAKE 173:

Dating a parent...

Earlier in the book, I dedicated a section to teaching the children of someone you are dating. That section assumed that you were already dating the individual before you had their child assigned to your classroom. I do not recommend that you start dating the parent of one of your students under any circumstances.

There are many reasons why this could be a complicated and needlessly stressful endeavor on your part, not the least of which is how you would relate to the child's other parent. If you find yourself growing interested in the parent of one of your students and you believe they return the interest, the school year goes by quickly. Once the child is out of your classroom, you can try to pursue a relationship at that time. But while you are teaching little Tommy or Sarah, go ahead and rule their parents out as possible romantic interests. This advice will protect you professionally and spare you from becoming the subject of the school rumor mill.

CHAPTER 23:
Continuous Improvement

As a teacher, you are a life-long learner whether you like it or not. You will be called upon to complete several hours of professional development throughout your career and be expected to continuously work to improve your performance in the classroom. You might as well begin this process in your first year of teaching and perhaps impress your boss in the process.

MISTAKE 174:

Not working on your classroom presentation skills...

Hopefully you are an eloquent speaker who does not get tongued-tied or find yourself at a loss for words. However, if you still need to improve your lecture or presentations skills, be sure to practice this as the year goes on. I am certain that you will be observed at times to evaluate your performance. When this happens, you want to make sure you are comfortable leading your classroom and free of verbal pauses and lapses. Since practice makes perfect, work on this with friends, in front of the mirror and perhaps even ask a mentor to observe your classroom before your evaluation to provide you tips and recommendations.

MISTAKE 175:

Not planning ahead...

In the first chapter, I reviewed how important it is to plan for the first day/week of school, but that is not where the advance planning ends. You will want to plan weeks in advance for delivering your curriculum and planning tests/special projects. You need to take a look at the school calendar and see how to fit your curriculum plan into the school schedule to make things easiest on the students. You do not have to have a plan so firm you never deviate from it – just make sure you are not making it up as you go along.

MISTAKE 176:

Not adjusting your lesson plan if needed...

If something comes up that you failed to anticipate, make sure you are willing to alter your lesson plan to accommodate needed changes. Whether this is due to children needing more time on the material or an interesting learning opportunity arose that you want to take advantage of. While it is vital to plan ahead, it is also important to be flexible enough that you can always put educating your students first.

MISTAKE 177:

Not adjusting your teaching methods if they appear ineffective...

Since you are new to teaching, it is reasonable that you will need to make changes to your teaching strategies throughout the year. There may be nothing wrong with your approach in theory, but it could just not be working for you and your students. Whether this is a change in testing strategies or trying a new approach in how you communicate a lesson, be open to trying something new if it will help your students better master the material they need to learn.

MISTAKE 178:

Not reviewing what types of questions your students are struggling with...

Every time you give a test, you have an opportunity to evaluate where your students are struggling on an individual level, but also as a group. If you find that most of your students are having a hard time with a specific type of problem, you should spend extra time reviewing that material and practicing how to answer those questions. If all you do is grade the tests and send them home, you miss an opportunity to improve your teaching approach.

CHAPTER 24:
Avoiding a Lawsuit

It is almost a shame that I have to include a chapter like this, but it is also easy to get sued in today's world (or at least threatened with a lawsuit). In order to protect yourself against litigation and disciplinary measures by your administration, avoid the mistakes laid out in this chapter.

MISTAKE 179:

Not knowing applicable laws for schools in your county/state...

Ignorance of the law is not a defense for breaking it. This common axiom is the reason why saying you did not see the speed limit will not save you from a ticket. Breaking the law at your school as a first year teacher will undoubtedly make it difficult for you to advance your career. Make sure you know the laws and regulations that apply to your school and make every effort to comply with them.

MISTAKE 180:

Not making students aware of risks, even ones you think they should know...

As foolish as it may sound, if you fail to make children aware of potential danger and they get hurt, you could be considered liable. Therefore, put some thought and consideration into what dangers your children face in your room and what safety rules you need to brief your students on. For example, even if you are sure they know not to run with scissors, go ahead and tell them not to all the same.

MISTAKE 181:

Not monitoring your students closely while they are in your care...

On a related note, be sure you keep a diligent eye on the children in your class. When they are in your care, if something happens to them, parents will hold you accountable. Be careful about stepping outside, allowing yourself to be distracted for an extended period of time, or focusing so intently on an activity that you lose track of what is going on in your classroom. Even if you allow your students some free time, keep an eye on them to make sure no one is doing something stupid or dangerous.

MISTAKE 182:

Purposely embarrassing a student...

I have detailed how being snide, sarcastic, or rude to a child is unprofessional and unlikely to achieve your purpose. However, you should be aware that embarrassing or harassing a child on purpose is also a good way to get yourself reprimanded or named in a lawsuit. If you are ever tempted to speak harshly to a student (no matter how justified it may seem), be cautious, bite your tongue, and keep silent.

MISTAKE 183:

Not removing a student who is dangerous to another student...

You know that you need to maintain a safe, bully-free classroom. If you feel that a student is starting to pose a danger to another child, do not ignore your gut feeling. Send the child to the office and report the issue to administration. Hopefully, your principal can take the needed steps to get the aggressor in line so that there are no instances of violence. While some old-fashioned parents might not blink an eye at a couple of boys getting into a tussle, many parents today would be very upset if their child was hurt at school. Do not let any such incident happen on your watch.

MISTAKE 184:

Not protecting a student's privacy...

In an earlier chapter, I advised against engaging in gossip in regards to your coworkers or student parents. When it comes to your students, do not discuss their private issues needlessly. If you want to seek the advice of a mentor and explain the problem you are facing with a student, try to do so without naming the child. In the instances where it is necessary to discuss the child by name, be sure that you are doing so for the good of the student.

MISTAKE 185:

Not complying with laws regarding incidents you feel are suspicious...

There are instances where you learn – or think you have learned – information that you are required to report to the appropriate authorities. If you think you are obligated to report something, but are unsure how to do it or who to contact, consult someone at the school who is qualified to advise you – a school psychologist, a mentor teacher, or your principal.

MISTAKE 186:

Not knowing your student's medical needs...

Hopefully your students do not have overly complicated medical needs, but if they are facing severe allergies or other potential health risks, you need to be aware of them and know what to do in the case of an emergency. This is doubly true if you are going on a field trip with your class. Do not take it for granted that all of your children are healthy as a horse – make sure you review their files for any information you need to remember throughout the school year.

MISTAKE 187:

Not documenting communications with parents...

On the slight chance a parent takes issue with you and calls you out in front of your boss, be sure that you have documented your communications with the parents well. This could be as simple as keeping track of emails and notes sent home to the parents of all your students. If you take care throughout the school year to document communications with parents, you will not find yourself needing to scramble later in the year if there is an issue.

MISTAKE 188:

Using a student's image without
their parents' permission...

This is pretty simple and straightforward – do not use images of your
students without permission. Do not post their images in your newsletters
or on a social media page. Do not use their image in any way without first
getting signed permission from a parent.

CHAPTER 25:
Impressing Office Staff/Your Boss

You never get a second chance to make a good first impression. Over the course of your first year of teaching, you want to make every effort to put your best foot forward. That is why you should be extra cautious to act in a professional manner at all times. In order to establish a good relationship with the office staff (who can make your life so much easier) and your boss, avoid the mistakes listed in this chapter.

MISTAKE 189:

Avoiding extra work...

Throughout this book, the teachers who were interviewed have stated things such as, "Do not get involved in campus politics" or "Do not get burned out." However, you still need to be "true to your school," so to speak. You cannot dodge school events, even if somehow they do not involve you or your students. You cannot avoid all PTA activities, fundraisers, and other activities and expect to be viewed positively by your employer.

While you do not need to volunteer or work yourself into the ground, it is smart to attend social events, eat lunch with your colleagues, and stop for small talk now and then. Additionally, if you can help a teacher out from time to time, you will find it easier to ask them for help if you ever need it. You are part of a team and need to prove yourself to be a valuable member.

MISTAKE 190:

Not being considerate when using copiers and office equipment...

You are going to need to make copies, send faxes, and use other front-office equipment as much as any other teacher. Just be sure that you are considerate while doing so. Follow whatever rules and procedures your school has for use of office equipment and pay attention to other people who may be waiting in line for use of equipment. If you have a lot of copies to make, let someone with a short stack move ahead of you. And try not to ask any of the office staff to move a huge stack of work for you.

MISTAKE 191:

Being overly defensive if a parent or student complains about you...

If a parent or student does file a complaint about you, defend yourself through documentation and approach the situation in a professional manner. Being overly defensive, argumentative, or emotional when speaking to your boss about an accusation against you will not help your case. Remain calm and reasonable and you can get your boss on your side, defending you to the parent or student. Any other approach and you might find yourself facing off against both the parent and administration.

MISTAKE 192:

Taking too many sick days...

As you make every effort to create a good impression with your boss, you should know that taking too many days off will not accomplish this goal. While sick days cannot be helped, do not take days off without good cause. Of course you do not want to go to school and give an entire class of children a bad case of the flu, but work hard to maintain good health (get a flu shot, take your vitamins, etc.).

MISTAKE 193:

Going over someone's head...

Whether you by-pass someone by making a simple maintenance request or purposely skip over someone you know is in your chain-of-command, there is not much you can do that will ruffle someone's feathers more than going over their head. While the situation may come up where this is necessary, do so with great caution.

CHAPTER 26:
Final Thoughts

A great deal of this book has been dedicated to flooding you with awful mistakes you can make in your first year of teaching that could leave a bad impression on your students, their parents, or your colleagues. I do not want to conclude this book without reminding you that your job does not have to be miserable or nothing but stress. You can have fun as a teacher and in the end, I hope you find it to be a highly fulfilling profession. Consider these final "mistakes to avoid" to make sure you still find some joy in what you do.

MISTAKE 194:

Not smiling...

Do not forget to smile. Even if you are having a bad day, try to remember to smile at your students. When you see them smile back, it will lift your spirits and improve your mood. Plus as much as you want to be firm – perhaps even strict – with your students in terms of rules and classroom policies, that does not mean you need to appear to be in a dour mood all of time. Go ahead and let them see you smile, it will do both of you good.

MISTAKE 195:

Not praising a job well done...

Do not be so focused on trying to raise skill levels and overcome areas of weakness that you forget to praise a job well done. Children respond well to praise. They eat it up. You should hand it out generously, but only for positive achievements. You can elect to praise them privately, publicly, or both. Just make sure you hand out praise to all of your students. If you look hard enough, you will find a reason to praise even the most difficult student, which could lay the groundwork to turning that relationship around. Additionally, if you do praise children well, it should make it easier in those instances when they need to receive correction from you.

MISTAKE 196:

Not using stickers and other visual rewards...

As often as you tell a student "well done," be sure to also give out visual rewards for doing good work. Children love to see positive stickers on their work and gold stars after their names. You do not have to give these out without merit, but make sure you dole out these little "encouragements" throughout the school year to keep your students' confidence up and let them know what they do well.

MISTAKE 197:

Getting Discouraged...

Though it can feel tough at times, being a teacher is an incredible position. You have the power to influence and mold young, developing minds. Bad days will come, but try not to forget why you became a teacher in the first place. These children look up to you for guidance. If you're passionate about teaching, it will help them be passionate about learning.

MISTAKE 198:

Not making friends among your coworkers...

You do want to avoid school politics and gossip and drama, but there is no reason why you cannot make friends among your colleagues. If things work out, you will be working with these people for years to come and you should have a friendly relationship with them. While you want to keep your personal problems away from work, do not be afraid to consider yourself friends with your coworkers. Working in a school is the same as working in any corporate environment – enjoy the company of your colleagues, but remain professional at all work-related events.

MISTAKE 199:

Not having any fun...

As strange as it might sound, failing to have any fun during your first year of teaching would be a terrible mistake. You will burn out and probably not want to return for another year whether you get an offer or not. Like I said in the introduction, teaching is one of the most difficult professions – if you cannot enjoy it, you should not be doing it.

BIBLIOGRAPHY

"About Us." About Us. Ed. Scholastic News Editors. Scholastic News, 1996. Web. 27 Oct. 2016. <http://election.scholastic.com/about -us/>.

Burruss, Jill D. and Kaenzig, Lisa, "Introversion: The Often Forgotten Factor Impacting the Gifted," Virginia Association for the Gifted Newsletter. 1999 Fall 21 (1).

Hancock, LynNell, "Across the United States, parents, teachers, and administrators alike are rethinking their approach to after-school assignments," Smithsonian.com, 2011.

Mason, D.A. & Good, T.L. "Effects of two-group and whole-class teaching on regrouped elementary students' mathematics achievement," *American Educational Research Journal,* vol. 30, pp. 328-360, 1993.

Orange, Carolyn, "25 Biggest Mistakes Teachers Make and How to Avoid Them, 2nd Ed." Corwin Press, Thousand Oaks, CA, 2008.

Silverman, Linda, "What We Have Learned About Gifted Children," www.gifteddevelopment.com (2014).

Stein, Nathaniel, "Leaded! Harvard's Grading Rubric," *The New York Times*, December 14, 2013.

Strauss, Valerie, "Harvard College's median grade is an A-, dean admits," *The Washington Post,* December 4, 2013.

CONTRIBUTORS

Brandy Mayer

Clerk of Courts,

New Orleans

Christian Langley

Former Teacher/Current Stay-
at-Home Dad

Hollis Townsend

Director of Technology Support &
Operations,

Young Harris College

Jenna Rew

Writing Teacher,

Gateway Science Academy
High School

Peggy Nix

Training & Staffing
Solutions Manager,

ABTSolutions

Sara Razaire

Volusia County Schools

Shay-Anne Matthews

Former Teacher,

Tavares Christian School

Stephen Klubock

Career Coach and Account Manager

Victoria Andrew

Writer/Teacher

INDEX

AUTHOR BIOGRAPHY

Kimberly Sarmiento is a writer, researcher, and educator who currently leverages a background as a college professor and journalist to provide readers with advice on teaching, career management, and self-marketing. As an instructor, she developed and led undergraduate courses such as *American Federal Government* and *Political Parties and Interest Groups* at Cameron University.

Ms. Sarmiento is a graduate from the University of Florida with a Masters in Political Science and a Bachelors in Journalism. Over the course of her career, she has written for three regional newspapers, authored two books and several blogs on career management, and worked with hundreds of clients on the development of customized résumés and cover letters.

Recently, Ms. Sarmiento has been engaged on a volunteer basis to provide advice to teens on how they can translate high school experience into résumés content for the job market or college admissions. In her spare time, she enjoys going to theme parks with her children and reading.